P✓SITIVE UNDER PRESSURE

HOW TO BE CALM, POSITIVE AND EFFECTIVE WHEN THE HEAT IS ON

Gael Lindenfield and
Dr Malcolm VandenBurg

Thorsons

Thorsons
An Imprint of HarperCollins*Publishers*
77–85 Fulham Palace Road,
Hammersmith, London W6 8JB

The Thorsons website address is: www.thorsons.com
Published by Thorsons 2000

1 3 5 7 9 10 8 6 4 2

A catalogue record for this book
is available from the British Library

ISBN 0 7225 3817 0

Typeset in Great Britain by
Rowland Phototypesetting Ltd, Bury St Edmunds, Suffolk
Printed and bound in Great Britain by
Omnia Books Limited, Glasgow

Dedicated to all our children,
who have helped us experience the similarity
between pressure and pleasure

CONTENTS

ACKNOWLEDGEMENTS

We are indebted to literally hundreds of people who have in some way over the last 25 years helped us both develop the ideas and techniques we have presented in this book. Some of these people have been teachers, mentors and clients from our professional worlds, but many have also been inspiring and supportive friends or members of our families. We just hope those people know who they are and know how grateful we are for their help. We also hope that they will give themselves an enormous 'pat on the back' for playing their part in developing our work and helping us to manage our own pressure so much more successfully.

Gael would particularly like to single out her husband Stuart who has given her unwavering emotional and practical support through the most difficult periods in her life. He has also spent many hours editing the manuscript of this book. This was an especially difficult job, as the book was written by two highly pressurized people who were collaborating 90 per cent of the time by either fax or email!

INTRODUCTION

Are you hungry for success in your profession, relationships, and life?

Do you feel that you have been served up with too much pressure to digest comfortably?

If so, perhaps you are already now suffering and struggling under stress. Maybe you are only too aware that:

You now have too much to do, too many people to please, too many people expecting too much of you, and you collude in it all and search out more.

Your enjoyment of the previously enjoyable is getting harder to achieve, as are your goals.

Your feelings of discontent, sadness and anger are increasing, while you get less success, happiness and contentment than you desire and deserve.

If so, it is time to make the changes which both your heart and your head know are right for you. It is time to harness your pressure and make it start working *positively* for you.

Our belief is that pressure need not have such a negative effect on you and your life. On the contrary, it can be used to stoke your emotional boiler in a constructive way.

You can use pressure as a fuel to *speed up* your attainment of a fulfilling, ambitious, happy and contented future life.

How This Book Can Help You

- It offers a **simple and workable model** of pressure and shows you how this can be applied to your own personal experience.
- It can be a **guide for your own journey** to greater knowledge about the destination you are seeking and the changes you currently want to make in your life.
- It will help you understand the **origins of human response to pressure**, and your own personal reactions. It explains the differences between your feelings (*internal* stress) and the circumstances and situations that trigger them for you (*external* pressure). You will learn how to separate the two so that you can then work on each separately to help you perform better and feel happier.
- It will help you recognize when the **positive effects** of your pressure are becoming weaker and start to impact negatively on your life and being. Armed with this self-knowledge you can adjust your life and your responses, and commit to change.
- It explains the **differences between acute and chronic stress**. You will learn how to work on each by applying immediate techniques to alleviate the former, while working in a more long-term, complex way to reduce the latter.
- It will **bring theory alive** by illustrating with many examples (especially from our own lives) and giving you a chance to put the self-help exercises into practice.
- It explains the **process of change**, and suggests easy-to-learn techniques to keep you on a committed path.

How Can This Book Help You Do *All* This?

First, it relies on the professional knowledge, skills and the training of both authors. As we are from different disciplines and have also both undergone several career changes, our joint experience and knowledge are unusually far-reaching.

Secondly, and more importantly, we are two people with contrasting personalities who have learned to thrive on pressure in (often) very different ways. We both share a tendency to seek out an excess of pressure and have developed our own particular skill sets and individual inner strengths to help us avoid the negative effects of stress. Neither of our journeys to this point in our lives has been easy. We have both suffered many 'cruel twists of fate' and made many mistakes en route, and have had to rebuild ourselves from the very jaws of disaster. When our paths happened to cross seven years ago, we found that, despite our apparent differences, we shared many common values and a deep commitment to helping others avoid the pitfalls which we ourselves had fallen into in the past.

Gael is a highly acclaimed personal development consultant and psychotherapist. She is the bestselling author of nine groundbreaking self-help books and now works regularly with the mass media. During her 30-year career in the field of mental and emotional health she has worked with a range of organizations including health services, small innovative charities and multinational businesses.

Malcolm is a Fellow of the Royal College of Physicians, a very successful physician, research worker and entrepreneurial businessman. He has spent many years studying pressure, measuring the quality of life and planning processes of change. He has now harnessed his well-honed research skills to explore and explain the theory behind this *Positive Under Pressure* programme.

We believe that the strength of this book is built not only upon the differences between our skills, experiences and personalities, but also upon the many similarities in our current values and

approaches to pressure management. Through working together
we have found we are able to pool our knowledge with great
success, and have been able to help people from many contrasting
worlds as a result. As our joint practice has developed, we've
found that our individual approaches are in fact complementary,
enabling us to devise a particularly powerful programme. You
will notice that it is drawn from many different disciplines. These
include traditional physiological techniques, psychotherapeutic
skills and management training resources, as well as some from
the Eastern religions and the new and growing world of self-help.

How to Get the Best Out of This Book

Although we have now moulded our diverse 'hotchpotch' into a
single, continuous theory and basic pressure-management programme, we want to stress that it should not be regarded as
being set in stone. It is essentially a 'nuts and bolts' course
with which we want you to experiment. We believe that all
pressure-management programmes must be tailored to meet each
individual's needs and style. So as you read this book we will be
presenting you with a wide variety of tips and techniques which
we hope you will mix and match to suit yourself. From time to
time you will be encouraged to put these to the test immediately
by completing certain exercises before reading any further. Once
you have done this, we suggest that you turn to the Endnotes
Section and jot down your own ideas, adaptations and comments
under the appropriate chapter heading. When you have finished
the book you can then review these and use them to help design
your own modified and individually tailored programme. You will
notice that on page 171 we have provided you with an outline
plan to help you do this over a period of a month.

Throughout the book you will also notice that we have highlighted certain statements which are written in the first person
('I' statements). If possible we would like you to read these
statements to yourself (preferably out loud). Doing so will help

reinforce your commitment to becoming *Positive under Pressure*, and set the section you have just read more firmly in your brain's memory bank.

We hope that you will find this book easy to follow and that it will be an inspiring catalyst to change. We are confident that if you apply our theory and your own chosen set of adapted techniques to your life, you will soon be able to be the best you can be and feel better than you have ever been, because you will know how to be:

Positive Under Pressure!

PRESSURE LEADS TO PLEASURE

If you were taught at the same school we were, you will already have read the pages that came before this one – for most of us were taught that books begin at the front cover. So you will have already noticed that the book is dedicated to our children, for helping us learn that pressure is closely linked with pleasure!

Of course there have been many, many times during our parenting years when the pressure felt far from pleasurable. In fact it made us feel extremely uncomfortable. We've had numerous physical aches, we've felt tired and despondent, powerless, and we've behaved in ways which we would rather forget.

In short, our pressure had given us *stress*, which is the collective name given to the negative effects of too much pressure. So we readily accept that pressure can become acutely painful, and can lead us to experience pain. But as you are working through this book, we would like you to accept that, when it is well-managed, pressure can also give a great deal of pleasure.

PRESSURE LEADS TO PLEASURE.

By the time you finish this book we hope you will have learned how to ensure that your inner 'pressure thermometer' will always indicate that the pressure you are under brings you much more pleasure than pain.

Many of you may remember the song penned by 1980s pop group Queen, 'It's a Kind of Magic', where they sang about pain being so close to pleasure, just like rainy weather and sunshine going together, hand in hand with each other.

It is our experience, too, that pressure can bring excitement. Excitement is at the root of some people's pleasure, but excitement is one step away from anxiety, anxiety from stress, and stress from emotional pain and even physical pain (stress can lead to migraine, heart pain, chest pain and joint pain, to name but a few. We will discuss this in more detail later on!)

The basis of feelings of excitement and anxiety are emotionally and physically similar. Both are based on the activation of our hormone system and the excretion of adrenaline.

Anxiety has been defined as the capacity to imagine pain. Pleasure is much more intense after first experiencing pain. The pleasure-pain cycle has also been thought to be linked to the process of addiction.

This may seem hard to understand at first, but we have found that some people, particularly high achievers, find the feelings of pressure pleasurable, and, as a result, subconsciously seek out pressure in their lives. As you are reading this book, it would be our guess that you are one of these people. We know that we certainly are. Once we accept that we seek out our own pressure, we can then take control of the situation and we can begin to choose when to seek it, as a way of beginning to manage it.

> I SEEK OUT MY OWN PRESSURE AND
> I CAN LEARN TO CONTROL IT.

Another important truth that we ask you to accept is that there is a difference between the feelings you experience and the situations that trigger them. The *feelings* of stress are *triggered* by pressure. If you are able to make this distinction between stress and pressure, this immediately gives you two *different* ways of coping:

1 Alter the external pressures.
2 Alter the feelings aroused by these pressures.

> I UNDERSTAND THAT THERE IS A DIFFERENCE
> BETWEEN THE PRESSURES *EXTERNAL* TO ME
> AND THE UNCOMFORTABLE FEELINGS WHICH
> ARE *INTERNAL* TO ME.

Making this distinction allows you to stop blaming other people, or situations for your *own* feelings. You stop saying, 'I feel stressed because my children are behaving badly at school.' You stop thinking, 'I am stressed because my husband is never at home.' You banish to the basement forever the thought that you are feeling stressed because there is traffic noise outside your house.

Once you stop blaming outside forces and take full responsibility for your own feelings, you are able to begin to alter them, without having to worry about the external triggering factors. You are able to relax while your colleagues pull their hair out, your children continue to misbehave, your partner stays in exile and the traffic continues to roar past your house.

> I WILL STOP BLAMING BECAUSE I AM RESPON-
> SIBLE FOR MY OWN FEELINGS AND I ACCEPT
> THAT I CAN ALTER THEM.

We assume that, as a reader of this book, you are very hungry for success in your chosen work and your chosen personal life. Please note how we have said your *chosen* work, and your *chosen* personal life.

Perhaps you *feel*, like many people, that you are not in a position to alter either. But of course the reality is that if these things in your life are causing you too much discomfort, you could walk away from both, provided you are willing to accept the consequences of doing so.

> I AM ABLE TO MAKE THE CHANGES IN
> MY LIFE THAT I WANT.

> I CAN WALK AWAY FROM ANY PRESSURES
> THAT ARE TOO MUCH FOR ME, INCLUDING
> MY JOB AND MY RELATIONSHIPS.

Now you could be starting to feel uncomfortable. You could even be beginning to sweat. We are not surprised (nor worried!) at this. We know that change can make anyone fearful. Indeed, one of the key secrets to making successful changes is to maintain the correct balance between fear and change.

This book will encourage you to make changes while showing you how to support your fears while doing so. This will, of course, be a skill for you to use throughout your life, because very few changes last forever and the bases for our fears are also constantly shifting. So, in order to keep the balance, not only do we have to continually monitor our plans for change, but we also have to inspect our fears regularly and check that they are still founded in reality.

> I've felt fear myself more times than I can remember, but I hid it under a mask of boldness. The brave man is not he who does not feel afraid, but he who conquers that fear.
>
> Nelson Mandela

There are many ways to go about altering your feelings. Practising relaxation, meditation, visualizations and positive memories are just some of the methods we'll discuss in this book.

Altering the pressures in your life means accepting that pressure is a mis-match between the resources you have and the demands placed upon you. You can therefore decrease pressure by reducing your demands and by increasing your resources. (There is a chapter devoted to each of these.) It is not only the absolute level of these which is important but how you perceive them. We therefore ask you to practise positive thinking to see your resources in the best possible light and to minimize the demands. Positive thinking also has direct benefits on your emotional health.

How is Pressure Management Different from Stress Management?

We have deliberately not used the title 'stress management' for this book or our courses. We believe that teaching stress management is like having an ambulance at every crossroads rather than traffic lights. The traffic lights are there to prevent accidents. The ambulance would be there to care for and cope with the results of accidents.

Similarly, stress management is a method for tackling the situation when it becomes a problem. Once you are stressed and in need of stress management, you are less able to know that you need help, less able to seek the help you need, and less able to benefit from the help once you have found it or it is offered to you. The harmful effects of your pressure are too advanced. You are into emergency care, rather than preventative care, and you are reacting to a situation rather than proactively managing it.

The concept of pressure management is that you learn to manage the pressures in your life and your responses to them, so that you are less likely to reach the point of stress. None of us is perfect, and this book will not, even if you did everything in it, stop you occasionally, if not frequently, reaching a point close to stress.

I WILL LEARN TO MANAGE MY PRESSURE
TO HELP MINIMIZE THE RISK OF
BECOMING STRESSED.

The ideas and techniques in this book are not, of course, magic wands. They are simply tools which, along with many others of your choosing, you can use to help you to keep a balance in your life. We both still sometimes wake up in the morning feeling worse than we would like, or respond to a pressurized situation like bristling porcupines. But we now do this very much less often, and when it happens we know we can quickly tame the porcupine. We can dip into our *Positive Under Pressure* tool-kit and dissipate the difficult feelings.

I ACCEPT THAT, DESPITE MY BEST EFFORTS,
I WILL OCCASIONALLY NOT FEEL AS GOOD
AS I WOULD LIKE TO FEEL.

In order to manage your pressure you must become super-aware of your own feelings and performance. It may help to imagine that you have an in-built thermometer gauging your levels of emotion and performance all the time. Imagine also that you have an in-built rheostat, or pressure valve. You can adjust this valve to either increase or decrease your pressure, depending on whether you want to increase your performance or decrease your uncomfortable feelings.

I KNOW I CAN ALTER MY PRESSURE WHEN
I BEGIN TO FEEL UNCOMFORTABLE.

In short, this *Positive Under Pressure* programme is designed to help you:

- find ways of varying the external pressures
- learn techniques to modify your emotions, behaviour and

physical responses so that you can control the effects of pressure.

Degrees of Stress

The degree of stress we have even during the course of one day can, of course, vary enormously. There is nothing wrong with some ups and downs – in fact, life would seem pretty boring without them! As we said earlier, everyone needs a certain amount of pressure to perform at their best.

Take a look at the following diagrams for a moment.

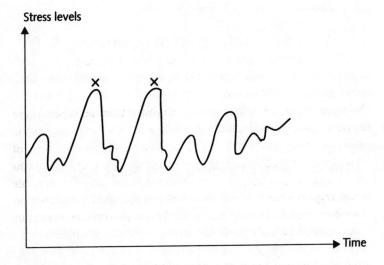

Stress levels

Time

The first diagram shows our stress level varying with time. As you can see it goes up and down during the day. Once we have reached the top of our stress curve (point X) we should routinely take immediate steps to reverse the trend by 'decompressing' our bodies. This is because they will have automatically started to function in emergency mode – that is, an aroused state of stress. The reason why it is dangerous to prolong this state is

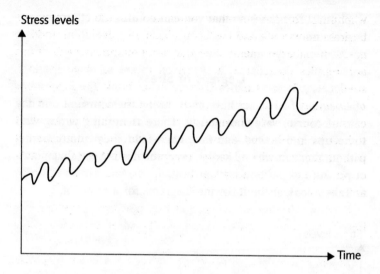

because if we do our stress levels continue to rise (see the above graph), with damaging consequences. This will become very apparent when in the next chapter we outline what actually happens to us physiologically if we do not.

The Origins and Functions of the Stress Response

Stress is a collection of physical and physiological feelings and symptoms which develop when our brains perceive a threat or a challenge. The uncomfortable feelings become stronger as we begin to use up our internal and external resources, and they get intense when we start doubting our ability to overcome the challenge or divert the threat.

Although everyone's experiences, responses and feelings are different, there is a common theme in the changes we experience. This means that everyone is able to relate to the general term 'stress', even though their individual symptoms will differ.

Across the boundaries of towns, countries, continents and civilizations, the core similarities of the stress response are overwhelming. This has led many people to believe that its origin is basic to human life and has been selected by evolution. Indeed, many animal experiments show that other mammals, birds, fishes and reptiles do react to a perceived threat or challenge in a similar way. It was Charles Darwin, in his book *The Expressions of Emotions in Man and Animals*, who first suggested that the emotional and bodily changes were so consistent that they had to have been inherited, and were almost certainly a fundamental part of any animal's make-up. (People who believe that plants cry or feel pain when they are cut maintain that these responses are a basic principle of life itself.)

So theory to date would suggest that the stress response was initially beneficial to our predecessors. It evolved in various adaptations as a means of maximizing our chances of survival.

But in today's world, some elements of the stress response are useful in some circumstances and inappropriate in others. The tractor with its large wheels works well in the field, but in the narrow streets of a village its lumbering pace causes a traffic jam. Similarly, a tank survives in battle because it has enormous tracks and a gun turret, but if this was taken to the centre of a city it would be a hazard. Thus, something inherent for survival in one time, place or circumstance can easily become destructive or unworkable in others.

For the stress response to be most evolutionarily efficient, it has to be constant, instantaneous and independent of all the other stimuli, emotions and bodily functions occurring at the same time. We need it to come into play instantly and without fault. This is why it has been developed as an automatic in-built reflex mechanism, over which we do have not conscious control. For example, if we are walking along a street and are approached by a gang of muggers, we need to have the same response on a cold drizzly day when we are depressed as we would on a sunny day when we are happy.

This in-built reflex which produces the stress response has become known as 'the fight or flight mechanism'. It earned its name because it first evolved in prehistoric times when these two survival techniques – fighting a threat or fleeing from it – were what we needed most.

The Body's Physical Response to Stress

At its simplest level, the fight or flight response produces an increase in blood pressure, accelerated heart rate, and sweating. (This is the basis of a panic attack.) It is controlled by our autonomic nervous system (ANS for short). This system works through a series of nerves which come from certain primitive sections of the brain which are physically distinct from those responsible for our more recently developed higher processes that direct our thoughts and more refined movements.

Our autonomic nerves run throughout our bodies and produce effects on all our various organs. At the same time a change takes place in our hormonal system which has an effect on our peripheral glands. These also help prepare us physically for fight or flight.

As all these physical changes happen, we begin to experience changes in how we feel. Our mood alters as we become more aggressive, waiting for the fight, or frightened as we shy away.

All these effects were normal, natural and productive 25,000 years ago, but they are not really helpful to the majority of 21st-century people. Indeed they are usually counter-productive and uncomfortable. Most of today's pressures do not require an immediate fight or flight response; they require us to stay put and THINK and CHOOSE whether or not we want to act in any one of an infinite variety of ways.

As an alarm system, our stress response can still be useful if it is kept strictly under our control. It is like a burglar alarm on the car which is programmed to go off automatically the minute somebody tries to break in. Of course, more often than not, it isn't a thief who sets the alarm off, it is us or a non-threatening accidental 'happening'. If we open the car doors, forgetting the alarm is switched on, we can find ourselves feeling as embarrassed and guilty as if we'd just been caught stealing! Similarly, we can feel very annoyed if a heavy lorry or a high wind shakes the car in the middle of the night and we are awakened by angry neighbours demanding that our alarm is silenced. But despite all these inappropriate triggers, we may still choose to have a burglar alarm. We need its protection in real threatening situations.

So it is with our autonomic nervous system. It helps us survive, but can be set off both accidentally and inappropriately.

> I ACCEPT THAT WHEN I HAVE TOO MUCH
> PRESSURE MY BODY AUTOMATICALLY
> SWITCHES ON ITS PHYSIOLOGICAL
> STRESS RESPONSE.

It is worth looking in more detail at the body's response to stress, as this will allow us to understand both why we feel as we do during a stressful situation, and why some of our responses can actually ease our discomfort.

Our autonomic nervous system is consistently monitoring the state of activity of all the bodily organs. It then modifies this activity to minimize any abnormal changes which could be dangerous. Its main job is to maintain the body in a state of balance. It achieves this by influencing the glands within the body and all the muscles not directly involved in conscious movement. These include those of the heart, the blood vessels, the whole of the gut (from the stomach through to the small intestine, large intestine and rectum), the muscles lining the airways going to the lungs, and the eyes, nose, liver, pancreas, kidney, bladder and our sexual organs. All of these organs and muscles need their activities to be regulated and co-ordinated unconsciously at all times, even when we are in a state of sleep or unconsciousness.

There are in fact two divisions of this autonomic nervous system. One is called the *sympathetic* nervous system, the other the *parasympathetic* nervous system. The nerves of both these systems originate in the most evolutionary and primitive part of the brain, between the top of the spinal cord and the cerebral cortex (the latter is the part of the brain that controls thought, consciousness and higher mental activities as well as movement).

The Sympathetic Nervous System

The system which is activated in the fight or flight response is the sympathetic system. It is immediately switched into a state of over-activity. Its effect on the heart includes an increase in rate and force of contraction, to increase the amount of blood circulating throughout the body. The blood vessels supplying the muscles also dilate to increase their blood supply and reduce the amount being sent to the skin and intestines. The net result is that the muscles receive more oxygen and nutrients necessary for energy, making us ready for action.

At the same time, the waste products of our muscle contractions are carried away more effectively (this is why we may break out in a sweat, for example). The net result of all this frenzied internal activity is that we are capable of being both stronger and faster. This is why people are able to accomplish feats at times of stress which they are not usually able to do.

The downside is that the lack of blood supply and constriction of the muscles of the gut inhibits the movement of our stomach. When the stomach stops moving, its contents stay there for longer than they should. Even if we have not eaten, the secretions of the stomach remain – with the net result that we feel sick or even vomit.

Simultaneously, our spleen contracts to put the blood usually stored there into circulation, and our liver releases glucose (blood sugar) so that this may be used as energy.

Elsewhere in our bodies there is also plenty of action. The direct effect of the stress response on the nose, and the airways to the lungs, is that they dilate. They do so in order to put more air into our lungs and feed our bodies with increased oxygen. To accomplish this task the rate and depth of our respiration increases. This extra respiratory activity not only allows us to get more oxygen into the body, but it also gets rid of the carbon dioxide that builds up when muscles are exercised. The downside of this chain is that, as many of you must know, during times of stress our breathing feels very uncomfortable.

Our eyes and facial expression are also changing. Our ANS stimulates our eyes so that our pupils dilate, preparing them for intense focusing. Our skin colour changes and our nose may twitch. These changes may signal to other people that our fight or flight response has been activated before we are even conscious ourselves that we are functioning in a state of stress. This is why people who know you well may ask you what's wrong, or may treat you differently or behave differently. When our relationships suffer at times of stress it may be because those closest to us react to these primordial body signs and body language.

Inside our head there are also of course many different 'happenings' taking place. The blood supply to the brain increases to support all the extra activity in the various centres which control the stress response.

The Parasympathetic Nervous System

The job of the parasympathetic division of ANS is to slow activity down, including that of the heart, the sweat glands, the salivary glands and the lachrymal (tear-duct) glands. It is often noted that when both the sympathetic and parasympathetic systems supply the same gland, organ or muscle group, they tend to act in opposite ways. The relationship between the two systems is, in fact, one of the reasons why our individual responses to stress can be so different from person to person.

Hormone Release

Although the most immediate effects of stress are all mediated by the nervous system, as we have said earlier, our hormonal systems are also affected. The most well-known hormones which are excreted during times of stress are called adrenaline and nor-adrenaline. Nor-adrenaline is the hormone that is the transmitter of the effects of the sympathetic nervous system.

Adrenaline has similar effects but can maintain these effects over a longer period of time. It too increases blood pressure and releases glycogen and glucose into the bloodstream, as well as helping the muscles utilize this added supply of energy. It causes blood vessels to constrict, which helps make the skin go white and will stop bleeding in an emergency. It also releases fatty acids into the bloodstream.

At times of stress the production of other less well-known hormones is also increased. These include those released by the pituitary gland at the base of the brain, which in turn stimulate the release of hormones such as one called aldosterone (which conserves salt in the body) and a group of hormones called glucocorticoids such as cortisone, which control blood glucose levels and other important metabolic pathways. The glucocorticoids do two additional things: they encourage fat to be laid down in the body, and they thin the bones.

An important side-effect of all this furious strengthening activity during this time occurs in our immune system, which becomes depressed to a level whereby the body is less able to stop or overcome infections. (We will discuss this effect in more detail later on.)

Why Is It Important to Reverse this Stress Response?

There is undoubtedly a serious physical price to pay if the emergency stress response is sustained for too long a period. Acute stress causes acute bodily changes, which fade when either the stress goes away or a technique – such as relaxation or meditation – is used to reverse the changes. It is important to reverse the changes because if you do not, your body will almost certainly suffer.

If the stress response is sustained, the body begins to think that the changes that have occurred are normal. The body has a number of mechanisms to maintain the body in a state of normality. This process is called *homoeostasis*. When homeostasis 'returns' the body to the state of stress, it will increase heart rate, blood pressure, adrenaline and nor-adrenaline in an unhelpful direction, even when you are at rest and not stressed. You therefore become consistently subjected to all the physiological and psychological changes that you don't want or need. If this state continues you will be in a general anxiety state most of the time and therefore be prone to panic attacks with only minor provocation. We need the periods of reversal of these abnormalities so that the body can re-learn to function in a healthy state.

But not only will your body be kept in a heightened state for longer than it needs if the stress response is not averted, the changes begin to cause structural abnormalities which may then become irreversible. The adrenal glands may swell, the blood vessels become thickened and narrow, and the stomach may become ulcerated. These structural changes add to the likelihood of diseases such as hypertension, heart attacks, strokes and stomach ulcers.

There are also a number of diseases which are much more likely to occur when the body is in a stressed state. These include allergic reactions from pollens, pets and food stuffs. Your skin is certainly more likely to break out in rashes and be itching when you are stressed, and skin diseases such as eczema and psoriasis are made worse. (It is interesting that hypnosis has been shown, when combined with imaging and visualization techniques, to reduce the size of the skin's reaction to an injection of histamine, the catalyst of many allergic reactions.)

Asthma is another disease which may be precipitated by stress or other psychological factors. Although stress does not cause asthma, it is certainly one of the predisposing conditions.

Heart pain and heart attacks are also more likely to occur when we are stressed. This is because the consistent narrowing of the arteries and the resulting likelihood of the formation of clots within the arteries means that the blood flow through the essential organs becomes lessened. Once the arteries are narrowed, the rush of adrenaline when you are anxious may therefore be enough to precipitate a heart attack.

High blood pressure is also precipitated and made worse by stress, as is migraine and a condition known as Irritable Bowl Syndrome or spastic colon, where you get alternating diarrhoea, constipation, abdominal distension and pain. Stress also makes the blood more sticky. This has even been shown to happen during short-term stress situations.

The other gut conditions which are related to stress are peptic ulceration and lesser forms of intestinal inflammation such as heartburn and indigestion.

A number of other diseases which are commonly linked to stress are diabetes and rheumatoid arthritis, though the evidence for these is less convincing. There is no doubt, however, that the ability of the body to fight infections and disease is decreased during times of stress. Analyses of the literature on many different conditions have shown impaired immunity at the time of stress, particularly when it comes to the number of cells circulating and the ability to fight infections. Even specific stresses such as marital stress have been shown to affect the immune system. Recent reviews of the literature have shown that we are much more likely to get infections at times of stress, which certainly fits in with our experience on our courses when people say that when they are stressed they get more coughs, colds and episodes of flu.

Positive/Negative Effects of Stress

In the table below we have summarized some of the potential positive (evolutionary) effects of the stress response, and the negative effects if it is sustained or over-used. Why not photocopy it and pin it up where you can see it regularly – it may help encourage you to take positive action!

Stress Response	Positive (evolutionary) Function	Negative Effects If Sustained
Heart rate increases	To increase blood flow to muscles so that we can run faster	The heart may beat very fast and become irregular. You may feel unpleasant sensations in the chest and get palpitations.
Force of contraction of heart increases	As above	You may feel palpitations in the chest.
Blood pressure rises	As above	Headaches can increase (may not be due to the blood pressure but to increasing blood flow).
Occasionally heart rate decreases	To enable you to rest and not be seen by your enemy	You may feel faint or dizzy and experience palpitations.
Blood vessels to the skin contract	So more blood can go to the muscles	You look white and cold.
Skin blood vessels occasionally dilate	To allow heat to escape from the body	You look flushed and get hot.
Blood flow to muscles increases	So you can run faster	Lack of blood supply to other organs such as the gut causes uncomfortable feelings.
Sweat gland activity increases, especially around the mouth, nose, armpits, hands and feet	To lose heat and also to give bodily signs of aggression in the face, and to help the release of pheromones which could scare your enemy	You feel uncomfortable, look funny; bodily odours may increase; you may scratch your nose – a body language sign of discomfort.

Stress Response	Positive (evolutionary) Function	Negative Effects If Sustained
Pupils dilate	To let more light into the eyes, so that they may function in a more sensitive manner, and to give facial body-language warnings to enemies and signals to friends	Produces staring eyes which may frighten some people and alter their response to you.
Nose dilates	To let more air into the body	Nose feels uncomfortable (this may be why people who are lying tend to touch their noses).
Airway passages to the lungs dilate	To let more oxygen into the lungs and carry more carbon dioxide out	The bronchi become more sensitive and may constrict spontaneously, causing asthma.
Salivary glands stop working	So that you are not hungry and don't need to eat	Dry mouth.
Gastric acid secretion increases	To digest food really quickly to provide energy from food that is already in the body	Heartburn and peptic ulcers.
Stomach either increases in motility or decreases in motility	Increased motility to get rid of the stomach contents. Decreased motility stops you feeling hungry	Feeling sick or abdominal pains.
Bowels become hyperactive	To clear the guts prior to exertion	Abdominal pains and intestinal 'hurry'.
Bowels become less active	So that we don't want to go to the toilet during a fight or when running	We may become constipated.

I ACCEPT THAT IF I ALLOW THE STRESS
RESPONSE TO BE SUSTAINED OVER A
LONG PERIOD OF TIME MY BODY WILL
BE DAMAGED.

Common Evolutionary Reactions to the Discomfort of Stress

Most people are not able to cope for long with the feelings of physical and psychological discomfort which the stress response produces. They therefore feel compelled to change their behaviour in an attempt to alleviate their 'symptoms'. Through evolution we have developed some instinctive direct action responses to help us do this. They usually involve one of three kinds of behaviour, each designed to put a stop to the pressure causing the stress response. These are often referred to as The Three Fs – Fighting, Fleeing or Freezing.

Fighting

When people go into Fighting the pressure mode, they become aggressive. Their threshold to stimuli decreases and they become tetchy and hostile. A minimal stimulus will cause an exaggerated response. The aggression can be directed towards a given circumstance, an individual or a group of individuals.

Fleeing

When people choose to escape the pressure, they go into Fleeing mode. This could involve leaving in either a physical or psychological sense. When we leave in a psychological sense we may daydream or suppress unpleasant thoughts, or lose concentration.

Freezing

When people choose Freezing mode, they will keep as still as possible so that the 'stressor' causing the pressure can't see or find them. In its psychological form, Freezing behaviour can induce a state of helplessness. When we are helpless we are generally perceived to be less threatening. Extreme forms of helplessness become hopelessness, which some people believe induces depression.

Other Responses

Other evolutionary responses include changing our eating or sexual habits. Some people eat less, others eat more; some go off sex, some become addicted to it. This is because the stress response can cause a decrease in both feeding and reproductive behaviour, but both eating and sex can alleviate the uncomfortable feelings. Indeed, one of the most effective ways to calm down our system is either to eat voraciously or indulge in sexual activity. And who hasn't experienced the tendency to drop off to sleep after at least one of these activities?! (You may be interested to know that there are good physiological reasons for doing both. After taking food, blood flow is diverted from the brain to the stomach to aid digestion, and the lowered blood flow and oxygen to the brain induces a sense of calm and somnolence. During sexual activity we secrete into our bloodstream two opiod-like substances called endorphins and enkephalins, which help the brain and body feel better.)

Another evolutionarily-developed calming behaviour is, of course, exercise. Fitness campaigns often highlight this benefit to encourage us. It is therefore now fairly common knowledge that a few hours in the gym will increase endorphins and enkephalins and leave us feeling 'high' – even if we still look larger than we might wish!

But there is a price to pay for using any of these behaviours too frequently as a means of coping with stress. In short, too much stress can make us become addicted to our coping mechanisms.

Addictive Reactions to the Stress Response

Now that we have become a more scientifically able and aware society, many people now turn to one or more man-made methods of altering our body chemistry which we now have available to us. Under pressure you may yourself turn to legally available drugs such as tobacco, alcohol or tranquillizers. An increasing minority will also turn now to illegal calming substances. As we all know, the danger is that we can easily become addicted either physically or emotionally to any one of these pharmacological props.

But let's not forget that addiction isn't the only problem associated with any of the stress-induced behaviours we have mentioned so far. There are many other dangers. If you eat too little you become thin and have too few vitamins and too little fuel for the energy you need. If you eat too much food you become obese, with all the harmful physical problems that brings, such as arthritis and heart trouble, or psychological problems such as bulimia. If you have too little sleep you are unable to function during the day, and if you have too much sleep you are unable to accomplish all you need to do. If you withdraw from sex your relationships alter, whereas if you become over-sexed and this becomes a driving force in your life, you create problems for yourself, perhaps giving up work to participate in this activity, having affairs, and allowing people to be abusive towards you.

Similarly, many of the pharmacological props have other direct harmful effects on the body. Smoking damages your lungs, heart, brain and bowels. Alcohol damages your liver and brain, caffeine damages your heart, and we have already talked about the harmful effects of extreme mood alteration.

> MY NEGATIVE RESPONSES TO PRESSURE
> ARE CAUSING HARM TO MY BODY AND
> MY RELATIONSHIPS.

But, amid all these dire warnings about the stress response, let's not forget its advantages.

The Advantages of the Stress Response

Pain has developed physiologically as the warning sign of danger. Its function is to motivate us to change. When we put our hand on the hot pan and feel the pain, we immediately take our hand away. If we did not feel the pain and left our hand there, we would get even more badly burned. Things that damage us cause us pain, so we move away from them. People who do not feel physical pain soon damage their skin, their tissues and their bones. In diseases such as leprosy, syphilis, severe alcoholism and diabetes, where our ability to feel pain is diminished or absent, fingertips, toe-tips and often whole limbs are lost because we have not moved away from the pain.

So, the pain that stress produces *can* be our salvation if we both heed it and make changes at this point. The changes we need to make will vary for each one of us, partly because we each have our own particular pattern of responses to too much pressure.

I ACCEPT THAT THE PAIN OF STRESS IS A SIGN
THAT I MUST TAKE ACTION TO MOVE
AWAY FROM IT.

How Our Individual Response Patterns Develop

Why is it that some people experience more pain than others when they are under pressure?

Why does this pain manifest itself in so many different forms?

Why do we also all adopt different means to cope with the discomfort it brings?

Some of the reasons for our differences lie, of course, in our unique genetic make-up. Many people believe that our emotions, drive, personality and responses to pressure are genetically determined. Psychologists have even developed tests now to measure these factors. However, genes do not guarantee the development of a particular response, they just increase the chances of it developing.

There are many other factors which determine the way we respond to pressure. The neural connections in our brains which carry the blueprints for our responses continue forming throughout our life. As each of us has a very unique experience of life, our pattern of response is also very individual. This is why gaining an understanding of what has shaped the significant aspects of your personality is very helpful. It helps motivate you to change.

So let's examine some key factors which may have led to the development of your unhelpful or downright harmful responses. As you read through these next sections you may find yourself identifying with some of the people we have quoted as illustrations. If you do not, we hope that their reflections may prompt you into remembering your own past influences. Please remember that:

The list is not exhaustive. You will probably be able to come up with many other examples of your own.

Your analysis does not have to be perfectly thorough. We suggest that you need only do enough 'navel gazing' to convince you that you are *still* being affected by your past, and that this needs to be kept firmly under *your* control. Insight alone can never help unless accompanied by action.

Possible Influences on Your Past Programming
Your Parenting

You have probably already given some thought to the effect your parents had on shaping your personality. After all, this kind of introspection has become one of the most popular hobbies of our times! But have you thought through specifically how the parenting you received continues to affect the way you manage your pressure? These quotes from people we have worked with illustrate some very common childhood experiences of high achievers, and may ring some personal bells for you.

My best was never good enough for my Dad. I guess I'm still after his approval, even today.

My mother was always worrying.

My Dad's response to pressure was to shout and scream. It was terrifying – I was determined not to let that happen if I had kids. I suppose that's why I hold in my feelings.

I could never be as good as my sister – she was always the star. Although I don't like to admit it, I don't think I'll ever be happy unless I'm some kind of star – that's part of the reason why I can never give myself a break.

I don't think either of my parents knew what being relaxed meant. Even on holiday they were always doing things. We had to visit people or museums or build sand-castles.

Our family prided themselves on the achievements of my grand-father. He was a famous runner. His photos, medals and cups dominated the house. Although nothing was ever said directly, I think my mother's greatest hope was that I would turn out to be like him.

My mother felt she wasted her life. She died full of regrets. I feel that I'm living for her as well as me.

My parents lived through the Depression and spent many years unemployed. Our poverty dominated my childhood. All the arguments seemed to be about money. It's no wonder that I live in fear of losing my job. And I can't say 'No' even when I'm asked to work ridiculous hours.

My mother always did everything for everybody. I drifted into being like her even though I know it sent her to an early grave.

My father is still a workaholic even though he is retired. When he comes to stay, he never stops. He's always looking for jobs to do for us.

My parents went short of luxuries and holidays to send me to
the best school – I couldn't let them down. Deep down I feel
that I still owe them something.

Of course there are pluses as well as minuses to be had from
this kind of parenting. History books and newspapers are full of
examples of people who have lived their 'parental scripts' –
perhaps at great cost to themselves, but with the result that they
have achieved fame and fortune or great breakthroughs for society.
Winston Churchill is often quoted as an example of someone
who had a life-long yearning for his parents' love, but never
received it. His amazingly driven personality undoubtedly enabled
him to lead his country, onwards, outwards and through the
Second World War to ultimate victory and ensured his place in
history. What it did also, however, was to create what Churchill
called his 'Black Dog' – the name he gave to his severe bouts of
depression and abiding sense of deep loneliness.

Similarly, the singer and actress Judy Garland was driven by
trying to please her pushy but neurotic parents. She achieved
phenomenal success and her recordings and films still give great
pleasure to millions all over the world. But throughout her glamor-
ous career she was crumbling internally. Her steady descent into
addiction and premature death is now a tragic legend which will
always overshadow her musical legacy.

With the skills of *Positive Under Pressure* you can choose to
keep useful aspects of your parental 'drivers', while losing the
harmful habits which you have inherited.

I TAKE RESPONSIBILITY FOR MY PERSONALITY.
I CAN CHOOSE TO KEEP, MODIFY OR
SUPPRESS THE INFLUENCE OF MY PARENTS
ON MY PERSONALITY.

Your Experiences at School and College/University

Some educational establishments are much more 'pushy' than others and can play a powerful role in shaping our attitudes and behaviour in relation to pressure.

> Our school was so competitive – I think that's maybe where I started the habit of comparing myself all the time to other people.

> There was this Maths teacher who terrified me – sometimes it is as though he is still shouting in my ear.

> I can still vividly remember the disappointment in my English teacher's face when she heard my exam results. I often think how proud she would be of me today.

Your Gender

In the culture and age many of us grew up in there was undoubtedly more pressure on boys to achieve than girls. But, for some people – even those of our own age group and background – we know the opposite experience was also true.

> My mother always worked and she looked after the eight of us plus doing all the housework as well. Only the girls were expected to help – my father was always in and out of work.

> When a financial crisis hit our family, the girls were taken away from their fee-paying schools but the boys stayed on. I don't blame my parents – they thought they were doing the right thing, but it put a lot of pressure on us boys.

> In my family all the men were waited on hand and foot.

Your Cultural Background

This can have a powerful effect, especially in the early impressionable years when your brain is setting some of its basic networks.

I was brought up in a very remote country village. Life was very laid-back there, so when I arrived in the city I felt I was an alien from another planet.

In our country, education is everything. The status of the family depends on how well the children do at school and what profession you go into. We were all expected to become doctors or lawyers.

Being black in a predominantly white school meant that we felt we had to do twice as well at anything before we earned respect.

I think being the daughter of a Jewish refugee undoubtedly had an impact. We lived in a kind of ghetto community, which always felt threatened.

Traumatic Life Experiences

Obviously traumas present great pressures. The amount you've lived through and their severity will undoubtedly have an effect on your ability to manage pressure and the kind of reaction you will have when you meet the next challenge or trauma. We now know that the stronger the emotion you feel at the time of a trauma, the more firmly the experience is set in your brain's memory archives.

I was OK until my divorce. I think I used work as a way of getting through. I started taking things home to do in the evening and weekends. I stopped playing tennis because I didn't want to go to our old club and I just drifted into working more and more overtime.

I was made redundant seven years ago and we nearly lost our house as a result. I just don't trust that any job will last. So I dare not let up at work, and now even my weekends are spent doing home improvements.

I ACCEPT RESPONSIBILITY FOR THE EFFECT
WHICH MY PAST IS HAVING ON MY PRESENT.

Finally let's not forget that the past is YESTERDAY as well! Some of your past programming could currently be being *reinforced* by your present surroundings. We have found that this is especially true for people working in the average professional office.

I work in an office where everyone drinks at lunchtime.

No one takes lunch-breaks anymore – just lunch-meetings.

Everyone does overtime – it is expected and it's getting worse. And all the senior managers are at the office at least one hour before we start officially – how can I say 'NO?'

We can all take heart from the fact that, however difficult our past has been, tomorrow can be a little different. One year's time can be quite different, and 10 years' time can be very different. The first step is to accept that if we begin to behave differently today, things *will* be different tomorrow.

TO HELP ME COPE WITH MY PRESSURE
TODAY I WILL REMEMBER THAT MY LIFE
WILL BE DIFFERENT TOMORROW.

LAYING THE FOUNDATIONS OF CHANGE

Can this leopard change its spots?

No, of course not. But he is choosing to sit calmly watching the world go by while potential prey graze in the distance.

Similarly, the bull on the next page cannot change the length of his horns, but he is choosing to charge angrily at the gate instead of ambling around the field and enjoying the sunshine and his female companions.

Many other leopards and bulls might behave quite differently in the same circumstances. But it is unlikely that any of these animals has given a moment's thought to the differences in their brothers' behaviours and feelings. It is also unlikely that they are aware that they are making a choice about their own behaviour and emotional state. (The market for self-help books for animals has yet to be discovered!)

As third-millennium humans, our position is very different. We have now been blessed with self-awareness and the capacity and means to make innumerable choices. If we don't like the image we see in the mirror, we can change it. We can dye our 'spots' bright red and green with all manner of chemicals, and change our 'horns' by cosmetic manicure and grafting. Even more importantly for our purposes of managing pressure, we can also choose to change or modify almost any aspect of our behaviour and feelings – even if we cannot change the 'field' we find ourselves in or the other 'animals' which inhabit it.

Hopefully you already accept that:

Some aspects of your own personality, behaviour and feeling patterns do need to be changed.

There is a way for you to be able to do this.

If you need your belief and resolve to be reinforced, you could spend some time repeating the following affirmations over the next few days before proceeding to work through this book.

> I ACCEPT THAT I AM IN CONTROL
> OF MY PERSONALITY.
>
> I CAN CHANGE.

In this chapter we will introduce you to four important key areas of preparatory work. We have found that if you work through the following four steps, the benefits of the *Positive Under Pressure* programme will have a much greater chance of success.

Step 1 Learn the most effective way of changing. On page 36 we introduce you to our own simple theory of the process of personal change, and introduce you to a stage-by-stage strategy.

Step 2 Reaffirm your belief in the positive power of pressure. On page 43 we share with you our own favourite way of doing this.

Step 3 Start living more positively. On pages 48–56 you will find some suggestions on what you can start doing immediately in your everyday life.

Step 4 Identify your early warning signals. On pages 56–65 you will learn how to develop your own individual 'pressure antennae'. As you know, central to our concept of pressure management is the idea of prevention. We have to learn when we are at the limit so we can take action to a) reduce our pressure and b) take control of our feelings.

Step 1: Learn the Most Effective Way of Changing

Although many thousands of books and theses have been written on the subject, we believe that the essential process of personal change and development is very simple. There are five main stages:

1 Want it.
2 Think it.
3 Act it.
4 Feel it.
5 Be it.

To illustrate how this process works in action, here is an example from Gael's own experience. It illustrates how she has successfully changed one problematic aspect of the personality which she inherited from her genes and early life history.

For the first half of my adult life I used to be known as a 'scatterbrain'. For those who are not familiar with this term, it is used to describe someone who is constantly forgetful and never remembers where they have put things. Their mind is always flitting uncontrollably from one subject to another, and they rarely register facts for longer than 5 minutes!

Despite the obvious inconvenience of this personality trait and the uncomfortable feelings of anxiety it produced, for many years I was not motivated to change it. Indeed, I secretly took some pride in it. I felt it distinguished me from most of my fellow mortals whose lives seemed so restricted and restrained by mundane logic and orderliness. My 'scatterbrain' trait was evidence that I myself was destined for an infinitely more interesting and exciting life as a groundbreaking creative thinker and artist!

My disorderliness had to bring me years of painful pressure and uncontrollable anxiety before I even **wanted** to change this aspect of my character.

Once my motivation was energized, I then had to keep its momentum going by obliterating the negative self-criticism stored in my mind with **positive thinking strategies**. These encouraged me to **act** differently. I began to behave like an organized person. I started to make achievable to-do lists, jog my memory with post-it notes and use my filing cabinets daily instead of at six-monthly intervals.

Eventually my anxiety waned as I **felt** more confident in my newfound habits and way of being. I ceased to be described as a 'scatterbrain'. Indeed, I began to find myself openly envied for **being** such a well-organized person!

But I know only too well that, although I have in effect changed a central aspect of my personality, my scatterbrain tendencies will still re-emerge if I allow my pressure to mount to an unmanageable level.

I WILL KEEP MY PRESSURE WITHIN
MANAGEABLE LIMITS.

We are well aware that the five stages in the process of change can take a long time. But the good news is that you have already taken the most difficult step. If you have started reading this book, we can assume that you are past Stage 1 – you *want* to change.

I WANT TO CHANGE.

Furthermore, if you are dutifully reading the affirmations which are running through our text, you are also well on your way to completing Stage 2 – you are thinking positively about your ability to change.

I AM CONFIDENT THAT I WILL CHANGE.

So your next step is to move into action. You have reached the crunch-testing time! To make your task a little easier, here are some tips which we and our clients have found to be invaluable to follow when trying to act on a resolution.

Stage 1/Want It: Write It!

In our workshops we ask people to do this on special cards which they can carry around with them for the next month and display on their desk or any other place where it will be regularly seen. You could do this by writing out your intention on a large poster and pinning it up on your front door!

Should you need more convincing, there is now scientific evidence that we can improve our learning ability by reading and writing at the same time. It is as if only reading something allows a stream of thoughts to go on in our mind. The writing fixes it there. It is like speaking into a microphone: the sound goes in but you don't hear it until you connect the microphone to a tape recorder or some kind of amplifier.

Two sensory processes occurring together are always better than one. Research has shown that students who take notes in lectures remember better than those who don't. Our teachers knew this instinctively when they made us write lines, and not just make a verbal promise to change!

Interestingly, the two stimuli do not always have to be linked. Many teenagers find they do their homework better if they play music at the same time. (While we are writing now we have made sure that there is some beautiful contemplative music playing in the background!)

Stage 2/Think It: Say It!

We have found that speaking simple sentences out loud, such as the affirmations which are running through this book, has a much greater impact on our brains than a jumble of good intentions whirring around inside our heads.

Of course, for novices, this behaviour may seem peculiar and anxiety-provoking at first. This is usually because it feels so similar to the kind of self-talk that is commonly thought to be a symptom of mental instability. So, if you do feel 'silly' or embarrassed, just remind yourself that the reality is that statements are not the same as the incoherent ramblings of someone whose mind is disturbed by psychosis or drugs, which is rarely positive and constructive and not under the full control of the person. You on the other hand are at liberty to choose to speak out in the privacy of your own bathroom or from the top tower of your local town hall!

Stage 3/Act It: Share It!

On our courses we ask everyone to tell at least one other participant what changes they want to and intend to make. This exercise is usually very reinforcing and supportive.

Occasionally, however, our courses do attract some cynics. These may be people who are firmly stuck in the rut of their victim role and have come along simply to collect further fuel to fire up their anger with the outside world. Because they have an investment in proving that our methods can't help, they often sabotage other people's attempts to make the methods work. So, commonly, if someone shares his or her good intention they predictably respond with examples of when and how they have tried that strategy and (surprise, surprise!) it failed miserably.

So, take care when you are choosing a friend with whom to share your intention. Avoid the cynics. But, beware – you may not know who these are until you start talking. It is an unfortunate truth that many people find that their nearest and dearest can be the worst culprits. The irony is that they may have encouraged or even nagged us to change in the first place! For example, they may say we should take the pressure off ourselves by being more assertive, but when it comes to saying 'No' to them more often, they can be less than supportive!

If this happens don't draw your sword or kick them out of the house, just put your energy into finding someone who can and will support you. Rest assured that if your family or friends truly love you, they will eventually welcome the less-pressurized you. On this count we again speak from personal as well as professional experience. We confess to having been guilty of being less than supportive of our loved ones' efforts to change, and both still vividly recall having our scepticism deservedly thrown back into our surprised faces!

Stage 4/Feel It: Commit to It!

As any successful businessperson knows, intentions must be backed up with a firm commitment to achieving realistic goals within a defined period of time. But often, the very same people forget that their personal resolutions need the same treatment! I am sure that you have heard many friends or colleagues return from their annual holiday full of motivation never to allow them-selves to get so stressed again. Two weeks later you may notice the old habits have set in once again. They are perhaps skipping lunch or making hurried excuses for opting out of the game of squash or tennis they promised you.

If this kind of scenario is ringing uncomfortable bells for you, try making a more formal style of commitment to change by setting yourself some target dates and sharing these with a sup-portive friend. Alternatively the commitment can be spoken out loud to yourself. On our courses we make participants write down their goals and share them with someone else. They are then signed, witnessed and dated!

But again, a word of warning concerning your friends! For this role, don't forget that you must have someone who is assertive and astute enough to confront you when you make the most plausible of excuses ('Something quite unforeseen turned up at work last week'/'My mother came to stay'/'The weather has been so bad', etc.!)

Stage 5/Be It: Question It!

Many people with whom we work have another very unhelpful script programmed into their mind. This is one which tells them that, once they have made a resolution, they must stick to it even if it appears to be working against them!

Although a degree of persistence is of course an essential virtue in any programme for change, we have learned the hard way that carrying through actions which we have begun to doubt only adds to our pressure load.

To stop this happening we have learned to constantly question the value of our goals and methods. If we find they are no longer serving our purpose, we quickly abandon them and start our step-by-step process again with a new intention.

> TO SUPPORT MY EFFORT TO CHANGE I WILL:
> WRITE IT → SAY IT → SHARE IT → COMMIT
> TO IT → QUESTION IT.

Step 2: Reaffirm Your Belief in the Positive Power of Pressure

As we have already indicated, although many people recommend that one of the ways of coping with the difficulties of pressure is to eradicate it completely from your life, we do not believe this is so. We believe that people like ourselves actually perform better under pressure, and this is one of the reasons why we seek it out.

We therefore don't recommend that you opt out of your life. A life of meditating in the hills or tilling the soil of a self-sufficient rural commune might suit some people. But we believe a radical 'downshift' would produce more stress for the majority of the high achievers whom we have met. Instead, we ask you to accept that you enjoy pressure and that it can be a positive force in your life.

We suggest that, whenever you feel uncomfortable with the effects of pressure on your feelings, remind yourself that pressure brings a great deal of good into your life.

> PRESSURE BRINGS A LOT OF GOOD
> INTO MY LIFE.

You could also remind yourself that you are likely to perform best under pressure. Much research has shown this to be true. For example, students are known to perform better in exams if they know they will have to repeat the exam or course if they fail. If uncomfortable feelings are taken away completely with drugs, performance decreases enormously. Beta-blocking medication, which reduces our bodily feelings of anxiety, has been shown to decrease exam performance.

This knowledge helps us to understand why many civilizations in the past have made mind-altering, sedating, anxiety-relieving drugs illegal. Substances which make people feel too comfortable diminish their drive to succeed.

> I UNDERSTAND THAT I PERFORM BEST
> UNDER PRESSURE.

Many people therefore, when they want to increase their performance, increase the pressures in their lives.

> I ACCEPT THAT I SEEK OUT ADDITIONAL
> PRESSURES TO HELP INCREASE MY
> PERFORMANCE.

So, if it is true that we seek out our own pressure to increase our performance, it has to be also true that we can either abandon situations which are causing pressure or choose not to walk into those pressurized situations which we know are coming.

It is important when you are feeling very uncomfortable, or even slightly uncomfortable, that you are able to remember that good often comes with pressure. The good comes not only from both the sense of achievement and the afterglow of satisfaction of a job well done, but also because the mind opens up to other possibilities at times of intense frustration with pressure, possibilities which are then able to bring both change and reward. We need to use the memories of these real-life experiences to keep us constantly reminded of this truth.

Malcolm uses this memory to reinforce his belief in the positive power of pressure.

> I once produced a series of courses for doctors to help them learn to do research to US standards, at a personal cost of some £25,000. You can imagine my sense of disappointment when the three other lecturers and myself found ourselves facing an audience of only four doctors at the Royal Society of Medicine. Each had paid £200 for the day.
>
> It was during a moment when everyone else was telling me how stupid I was, that I had an idea. I decided that I would record the lecturers' speeches and then produce the edited transcripts as a book. The book then sold 50,000 copies in French, German, Italian, Spanish, Russian and Hungarian, and the ideas are about to be put into a new book in India.

Gael has a similar personal story:

> Just prior to the recession of the early 1990s, I set up a personal development centre in southern Spain, at considerable cost to myself and my family. This was the realization of a long-held dream. I had always longed to work with my clients in a beautiful, peaceful but also inspiring environment.
>
> For several years I thoroughly enjoyed living my dream and

it had also proved an exceedingly successful way of helping my clients. But then came an unforeseen setback – a recession. As this gathered its momentum in the late 1980s, people in Britain understandably panicked about potential redundancy. Personal development holidays in the sun suddenly became a luxury few could afford.

You can imagine the deep disappointment I felt as I noticed course bookings diminishing. My ideal way of working had proved effective, but through no fault of my own it now seemed doomed.

So I took myself off to my empty retreat to lick my wounds and ponder on a new way of earning the keep of our beautiful retreat. While sitting one morning on the patio soaking up the peace and sunshine under a brilliant blue sky and the cascading brilliant pink bougainvillea, I had a new idea. I decided that I would start recording cassettes. These would provide a much more affordable way of providing the help which I knew so many people still wanted.

On my return to Britain my publishers turned down my idea, but I persisted in my belief that there was a market for cassettes like this. I therefore decided to take a further financial risk and market and sell them myself.

The cassettes were an immediate success and I was comforted for the loss of my holiday project by knowing that I had found another enjoyable and perhaps even more useful way of working. A year later, my publishers decided to enter the market themselves, and I have now recorded a further six cassettes for them and we have plans for many more.

I am now aware that my holiday course dream had the potential to help but a few hundred people. I believe that my cassettes will probably help millions. Moreover, I am thoroughly enjoying making the recordings and the freedom my new, more flexible work programme gives me.

Now on occasions when I sense that I am about to become daunted and depressed by pressure, I use my imagination to recall the crucial turning-point in this story. I visualize myself sitting under the bougainvillea in my garden in Spain. I feel the warmth of the sunshine and see vibrant pink clouds above my head against the deep blue sky. I also recall the smell of the fresh spring air and the sound of the birds and crickets. This vision alone is often enough to restore my energy and faith in the truth: a setback can become a success if you think and act positively when under pressure.

We are well aware that you may not be able to recall such similar experiences in your professional life. However, we are sure that you may have a story from your personal life which could be just as effective. Here is another example from Malcolm which we have found has rung bells for many people.

When I was 15, and less fit than I would have liked to be, I was made to run the 1-mile race at my school sports day. (This was only because all the good runners were doing the sprints and middle-distance races.) Despite my fear and trepidation, and the weight of responsibility I felt for my team, I ran faster than I had ever run before. Amazingly, I came third in the race and helped my team win the athletics shield. I can still vividly recall my feelings as I crossed the finishing line. I see my father's smile, my mother's proud face, and the surprised eyes of the House Master. I can hear the sound of the younger boys in the team cheering, and my friends clapping. I can smell the new-cut scent of the bright green grass, and can even feel the heat of the sun that was shining on that warm summer's day. Just recalling my inner sickness at having exerted myself so much is still a source of reassurance. It reminds me of what I can achieve when under pressure.

Recently on a course, a doctor described how when she first had a baby she unluckily experienced post-natal depression. She found it very stressful to care for her baby and her patients in a busy medical centre. One day on her way to work she slipped and broke her wrist. Interestingly, this added pressure and the crises it brought proved to be her turning-point. It was the stimulus she needed to make many positive changes in the way the centre was run. As the centre began to flourish, her self-esteem returned. The positive memory she recalls is one day when she went to work with her baby cradled in her now-mended arm. She recalls the smiles, congratulations and all the cooing noises from her normally grumpy receptionist!

Essentially what we do with these happy memories is create a new set of blueprint responses in the neurological pathways in our brains. We are then consciously using these to trick our minds into believing that we and our world are OK, even though the problems may not be fully resolved. Because we are feeling good, we find that we feel more confident and start to think more constructively and creatively. We are therefore radically improving our chances of finding a solution.

> WHEN I AM UNDER PRESSURE AND FEELING
> BAD, I WILL REMEMBER THAT PRESSURE
> CAN BE GOOD, AND CAN BE A SOURCE
> OF CREATIVITY.

Recalling a positive memory works on many levels. You remember that:

You felt bad, yet survived – and therefore will survive again.
The stimulus went away – and so the current one will, too.
Your circumstances changed – as they will yet again.
Good emerged from a stressful situation – and can do so again this time.

> I WILL REMEMBER THAT MY PRESSURES
> AND BAD FEELINGS ARE TEMPORARY –
> I WILL SURVIVE.

Now it is your turn.

ⒺXERCISE

1 Recall a memory of a time when you achieved a remarkable success while under pressure, and then felt satisfied, elated, or content. Try to bring the details of the scene to mind by asking yourself the following kinds of questions, using the present tense:

- What kind of day is it?
- Where are you exactly?
- Who are you with?
- What colours surround you?
- What sounds can you hear?
- What shapes are you noticing?
- Can you smell any scents?
- Is anyone speaking? If so, what words and tones of voice are they using?

2 Recall the feelings you experienced. Note the sensations in your body which accompanied these feelings. Try to re-experience these while you re-run the scene in your mind.

3 Recall the success that you achieved and the feelings of pleasure and pride you felt.

4 Talk about the event with a friend, and during this time try to add more detail and feeling to the story as you do so.

5 Write down a couple of sentences which summarize your experience on a card. Look at this card from time to time over the next few weeks. Recall and re-live the sensations of your experience each time. The more often you do this, the more quickly the blueprint will become established in your brain. You will soon find that you can respond instantly with positive feelings to your remembered image.

6 Use your memory to inspire you whenever you are under
   pressure and begin to feel hopeless.

> WHENEVER I AM UNDER PRESSURE, I WILL
> TRY TO CREATE A NEW OPPORTUNITY
> FOR MYSELF.

Step 3: Start Living More Positively

We hope that you are already aware that, in order to help
yourself to stay positive under pressure, you may need to make
some changes in your lifestyle. So let's look at some simple actions
you could take which would ensure that your lifestyle is as
conducive as it can possibly be at this moment in your life.

Do More (or Better) Physical Exercise

Most people on our courses freely admit that they should do
more exercise. They know that they perhaps sit at their desks for
longer than they should, and they frequently confess to using
their car, taxis or public transport when they could easily walk.

Aerobic exercise is good because it builds fitness. We get a
stronger heart, better blood flow and an improved ability to carry
oxygen in the blood. Our blood pressure lowers and the heart
rate falls. We rest and are fit. Anaerobic exercise builds muscle
bulk and strength. It is also therefore good because it increases
our ability to use energy, burn our food and clear our blood of
dangerous fats. Moreover, we become slimmer!

As neither of us now plays sport regularly and exercise routines
have always been difficult for both of us to maintain, we are
always greedy for new, inspiring ideas. We are especially keen to
hear about those which we can integrate very simply into our
everyday lives. Here are some of the tips we have found helpful.
We hope there may be a few which may help motivate you if
you are in need of a little 'push' in the right direction.

- Make it a rule never to take your car or a taxi up to certain distance (e.g. 1 kilometre).
- Leave the car at home one day a week and walk or use public transport instead to get to work.
- When you visit the supermarket, make a point of parking in the furthest corner away from the entrance, which immediately relieves the pressure of having to fight for a parking space in the most popular area, and possibly the pressure of parking in a narrow space, and gives you the benefit of a walk to the supermarket and a walk back to your car with the weight of your shopping afterwards.
- Always use the stairs when there are one or two flights to climb.
- Treat yourself to at least two sessions once a year with a personal trainer. (If you can afford more, so much the better.) The first session would probably enable the production of a new personalized fitness programme for you, and the second could be a follow-up to check that you are keeping to the programme and it is being effective.
- Do your exercise in the company of others. Although exercising at home has many obvious advantages, most people find it much easier to stick to routines if they are with others (especially those who are obviously enjoying the experience!). This is why aerobics classes are so popular.
- Make your exercise as much fun as you can – dancing or playing a sport is usually much more appealing than the treadmill. (Though it does depend, of course, on who is on the exercise bike in front of you!)
- Acquire an assertive, lively dog who demands several long walks a day (Gael's best tip!)
- Walk while you talk with your family. Instead of sitting down to discuss ideas for a holiday or a worry about the children, talk about it while you all go for a walk. The exercise will stimulate your brain and help you to think more creatively.

- Join in your children's activities more often – their energy and enthusiasm will be sure to stimulate you. So, instead of dropping them off to play in the park, or watching them from a deckchair at the beach, ask to play with them.

I EXERCISE AT LEAST THREE TIMES A WEEK.

Improve the Quality of Your Sleep

Sleep is important because it both gives the body a period of recovery and allows important 'sorting' psychological and emotional processes to take place (such as happens when we dream).

If our sleep is disturbed we suffer physically, emotionally and psychologically. Our sleep needs to be of a regular pattern. The body has an inherent biological rhythm which is much less active at night and works best if our sleep pattern is in tune with the rhythm of our brain, hormones and bodily organs.

Many people we meet on our courses regularly admit to staying up too late and getting up the minute before they have to go out. They are therefore usually falling asleep from exhaustion and trying to get their bodies going again before their biological clocks are ready for it. Others find they have difficulty getting off to sleep, or repeatedly wake in the early hours of the morning.

If you share any of these problems, try some of these suggestions:

Exercise vigorously during the day, but never during the two hours before bedtime.

Establish and stick to rituals. Go to bed at the same time and do the same activities in the same order (e.g. 1/check doors, 2/put out cat, 3/clean teeth, 4/read book, etc.). Your brain and body clock will recognize the pattern and start producing sleep chemicals.

Avoid alcohol and caffeine for six hours before going to bed. Instead, drink something containing a natural sedative such as milk or camomile tea.

Snack lightly on a carbohydrate food half an hour before retir-
   ing. Avoid protein, fat, spices and any food which your body
   finds difficult to digest.

Relax tense muscles in a warm (but not hot) aromatic bath.

Stretch any muscles which still feel taut (preferably to some
   soothing rhythmic music) before getting into bed.

Write down worries on a pad beside your bed. Refocus your
   mind onto a tranquil scene.

Avoid watching a stimulating movie or news debate before
   bed; save these for during the day or early evening.

Watch Your Diet

We have found that few people on our courses are giving themselves a good enough diet. We would recommend seeing a nutri-
tionist if your energy levels are very low. Alternatively, there are
now many books available on this subject. In the Further Reading
chapter we have recommended an excellent one.

But perhaps, like us, you just need a gentle reminder from time
to time to take your diet back on a healthier track. So here it is!

Foods You Can Eat Freely

- Those high in fibre, such as wholemeal bread. This is a
  must to improve one's health, as is increasing the amount
  of fibre in your diet.
- Fruits
- Low-fat foods
- Fish (especially good for brain-workers!)
- Avocados, bananas, dates, etc. (all supposed to increase our
  serotonin levels and make us feel happier)

Foods You Should Eat Sparingly

- Fried foods (if you must use oil, make it virgin olive oil)
- Foods with unnecessary added sugar (many marked 'no
  added sugar' on the label have an excess of other carbo-
  hydrates or fats, so be careful)

- Packaged meals (those marked 'low fat' are usually high in sugar)
- Fattening fruits (for example grapes and cherries are high in sugars)
- Fattening vegetables
- Mayonnaise (and all similar fattening sauces which have a high content of fats, oils or butter)
- Cream
- Shellfish (very high in cholesterol)

I WILL BE CAREFUL TO BALANCE
MY FOOD INTAKE.

Engage in More Re-balancing Activities

As your lifestyle is undoubtedly a hectic one, it is very important to make sure that you realign the balance of your physiological state by switching from high tension to low tension at least two to three times during the day.

In the chapter entitled 'Relax', we give many examples of how you can do this by using methods such as physical relaxation exercises and meditation. In the chapter entitled 'Renew' we will also discuss the importance of integrating activities into your lifestyle which refresh your inspiration and motivation. Many of these activities will also help you to re-balance your physiological state.

I COMMIT TO TWO PERIODS OF MENTAL
AND PHYSICAL RELAXATION A DAY.

Soothe Your Senses

Many people's daily environment is stressful on their senses. To remain positive under pressure we need to take steps to ensure that these daily stresses are counterbalanced by soothing experiences.

We have all been programmed by evolution to respond automatically in various ways to different sensations. We can use this inheritance in a positive way to feed our senses with experiences which will calm us and uplift us rather than depress or agitate us.

Let's look at a few examples of positive experiences many humans have shared for centuries.

Colour

We all recognize red as meaning danger and excitement, and get scared at the yellow-and-black striping of a bee. Similarly, most people will be calmed by soft yellows, blues and greens.

Smell

Smells can also either be exciting, worrying or calming. Some we are conscious of and some, called pheromones, are responded to subconsciously by our bodies. Religion has known for a long time that smell can enhance mental sensation, which is why so many practise the rite of burning incense. Recently, smells have been shown to alter the level of the body's immunoglobulins, so there may be a good scientific explanation of aromatherapy yet to come.

Sound

High-pitched continuous sounds such as a ringing bell, a siren or the scream of a baby alert most people. In contrast, light rhythmic sounds such as the sound of gently rippling waves and waterfalls can be soothing, reassuring and relaxing.

Light

Bright light stimulates the chemical activity of the brain. We are programmed to wake to the bright light of dawn, and to rest when the sun darkens the sky. So dim light is generally associated with calm. This is why churches have traditionally been designed to be dark, and why perhaps in today's stressful world there has been such a boom in the candle market. (Can you imagine the effect of using these to replace the fluorescent tube and halogen spots in our offices?!)

Touch

When our bodies are shoved and pushed we instantly respond with negative feeling and our pulse rate soars. Gentle stroking, on the other hand, should have a naturally calming effect on both those who give and those who receive. Massage is good for you physically and emotionally.

Symbols

Evolution has given us many universal symbols which have the power to produce contrasting feelings. Just think of the different emotions which are aroused by a picture of a serpent or a dove, or the shape of a circle or triangle, or the sketch of a winding path compared to one drawn as a zigzag.

Of course there are exceptions to all the above rules. We have found that some people:

find red a wonderfully relaxing colour to have in their
    bedroom
feel claustrophobic in dark churches
become irritated when they are stroked
associate rippling brooks with loneliness and fear.

What we need to do, of course, is to identify (and use!) what works best for us in each of the above categories. You can then use these to help you to maintain the mood you want and require when you are under pressure.

When we run courses we play certain sounds and music, generally considered calming, for our participants, but we also include other pieces which have personal significance for us and we know will give our own spirits a boost. We have also consciously chosen the 'corporate colours' of *Positive Under Pressure* – dark blue and turquoise – to arouse the feeling responses we desire in both others and ourselves. Dark blue is reputed to send out signals of confidence and professionalism. Turquoise happens to be a personal favourite and has warm, relaxing associations for us.

The singer Luciano Pavarotti is a man whose life must be more pressurized than most. Although he has many years' experience of coping with his lifestyle, he still carries his large white handkerchief with him to all his performances because it has a calming influence on him. Similarly, Malcolm has had very many years' experience of presenting courses to thousands of people all over the world, but even if he is presenting to an unthreatening group of 12 friendly doctors he still wears something yellow (because this is a colour of special significance for him) or one of his many hundred elephant ties. He has 'adopted' this animal as his personal symbol because he associates it with qualities of strength, gentleness and perseverance, which he believes are crucial in his role as a trainer in our field.

We have designed the following exercise to help you to commit to improving the quality of your life *immediately*.

❷XERCISE

1 Note down one way in which you will provide more or better exercise for your body over the next month.

2 Make a vow to do something to improve the quality of your sleep.

3 Make a note of two foods which you promise to give more to your body in the next month, and two you will avoid.

4 Look around the room you are in at the moment and choose two colours which have positive associations for you and two which you do not like. Notice which of these two groups of colours are dominating the overall colour scheme of the room.

5 Think of a smell which immediately makes you feel calm

and at peace. Picture the scene you associate in your mind with this smell. Note the relaxing effect on your body.

6 Name one piece of music and one other sound which have both a positive and an energizing effect on you.

7 Think of a way in which you could alter the lighting in your home or office to make it more conducive to relaxation.

8 Choose an object, picture or shape which could symbolize the concept of being *Positive Under Pressure* for you. Draw it on a card or piece of paper and carry it around with you. Alternatively, pin it up somewhere you'll see it often.

Step 4: Identify Your Early Warning Signals (EWS)

Most people who attend our courses can readily tell us how they feel and behave when they have reached a stage of extreme stress. Here are some examples of the symptoms they have reported. Perhaps some will sound uncomfortably familiar to you.

I start having panic attacks before meetings, and I am normally such a confident person.

I become impossible to live with – I snap at everyone.

I can't sleep.

I want to sleep all the time – I start to walk around like a zombie.

I get violent headaches.

My back gives in and then I have to lie flat for three weeks.

I start driving really badly. I narrowly missed having a serious accident last week.

I get continual indigestion.

My memory goes – I can't remember where I have put anything.

Why is it that so many intelligent human beings allow themselves to reach a point where they experience so much pain and put their jobs and relationships at risk?

Why do so many high achievers commonly need these kinds of crises before they accept the reality of what has been happening to them over an extended period of time?

We believe that the vast majority of these people are not inherently self-destructive. In fact they often feel very 'silly' about having allowed themselves to reach such a stage. It is not what they want, consciously or unconsciously. They cannot understand how it could have happened. They are people who are usually very astute and observant, but in this respect they were blind. They were not aware of the damage they were doing to themselves. On the contrary, if you had asked them just before the crisis 'How are you doing?' they may well have promptly responded, 'Absolutely fine, never felt better!'

This is such an important point for us all to bear in mind. Up to a certain critical stage, high achievers get pleasure from pressure. It pushes us to perform at our best. In the 'high' of the experience even the most humble among us becomes somewhat grandiose. With the adrenaline pumping through our bloodstream we become totally confident of our physical and mental abilities. The more we have to do, the more energy we seem to find.

We have no trouble understanding why people say, 'If you want something done, ask a busy person,' because we are those busy people. And, of course, we don't doubt that we can always fit in that little extra task or two. Experienced crafty manipulators know this too. They have a sixth sense for sniffing out when we are in this state. Unscrupulous bosses will pile on the work, and cunning children will extract extravagant promises from their benevolent parents.

So, addicts of the thrills of pressure must defend themselves not only from their own sense of omnipotence and but also from others who may abuse them because of it. The key to doing this is to stop the problem from developing in the first place. In effect, this means stopping it in its earliest phase, *before* it causes any real pain or discomfort.

The task of doing this would be so much easier if we had been equipped with an in-built pressure gauge. Perhaps one distant day, evolution may spot the survival advantages of such a tool, but for the moment we will have to make do with our imagination!

So imagine for a moment that, like your central heating system, you have a gauge with a graph like the one in the illustration opposite.

Note that there are two lines on the graph:

1 Indicates the state of your performance (straight line)
2 Indicates the state of your feelings when you are under pressure (dotted line).

I WILL LEARN HOW TO KNOW WHERE I AM
ON MY PRESSURE PERFORMANCE CURVE.

Notice how the shape of the performance curve illustrates that:

Increasing pressure leads to increased performance. This is
    part A–B of the curve.
There is a point at which pressure stops enhancing perform-
    ance (as shown between points B and C of the curve).
    When the pressure reaches beyond point C, performance
    starts to deteriorate.
Initial deterioration is slow (without great harm) shown as
    C–D.
At a certain point (D), performance starts to descend rapidly to
    the point of burnout.

High achievers who seek out pressure in their lives learn (consciously or unconsciously) that they perform best when under
pressure, providing they are on the A–C portion of this curve on
their imaginary graph.

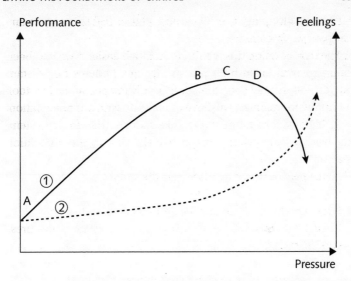

I UNDERSTAND THAT I PERFORM BEST UNDER
PRESSURE AND THAT MY PERFORMANCE
INCREASES AS MY PRESSURE INCREASES.

You will note that in this graph the feelings line doesn't begin to rise until the performance curve has started to drop – and even then it rises only slowly at first. This is because this graph represents a high achiever who enjoys pressure and can tolerate it without feeling very bad.

The graph on the next page illustrates the kind of feelings curve you might see on the graph for someone who feels stress after only minimal pressure. Notice that it rises steeply while pressure is still low.

As we haven't been equipped with a handy pressure gauge and cannot see what is happening to our feelings and performance curves, we must find an alternative way of monitoring them. The simplest and easiest method we have found is through identifying our own personal Early Warning Signals (our EWS, for short!)

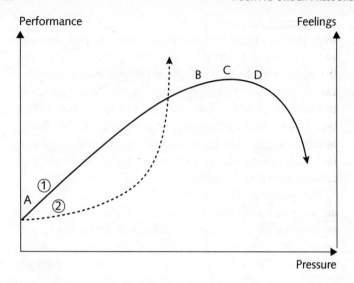

These are slight changes in either our body, emotions or behaviour which indicate that we have begun our descent down the slippery slope towards stress.

We use these signs to alert us to the fact that it is time to adjust our pressure valves – even if we are currently feeling great and we can see no sign of even a mini-crisis on the horizon.

Here are some examples of our own signals in each of the three areas: physical, emotional and behavioural.

Gael's Early Warning Signals

The physical signal I watch for in my body is a *slight pulling sensation behind the right eye*. This is a weak area of my body because I have chronic problems with the functioning of my sinuses, and also in recent years have had an attack of shingles of the right optic nerve. If I were to ignore this EWS I know from bitter experience that I would almost certainly suffer painful headaches and eye strain. A little later I could expect a disabling attack of sinusitis coupled with blurred vision in my right eye.

My emotional signal is a *mild attack of pessimism, tinged with anxiety*. I begin to have doubts about the possibility of a good outcome of whatever I am attempting to do. I might notice that I expect my train will be late and I'll miss my appointment. Later I might hear myself talking about how hard I am going to find it to write the next chapter, and then won't start it because I am too busy worrying about my well-travelled daughter who has just taken to the air again. If I were to ignore this EWS, and pile myself up with more pressure, I would most certainly slide into depression.

The special sign which I have learned to look for in my behaviour is a *failure to clear the top of my desk* at the end of my working day. I have already spoken about my problem with organization; this behavioural signal surfaces when I am not managing my pressure well.

Malcolm's Early Warning Signals

When I have allowed myself to get stressed in the past, I have developed Irritable Bowel Syndrome. This is a very painful condition and completely disrupts my normal everyday life. I have traced the very first sign of this condition to a change in my body temperature. When the problems are starting *I become a little warmer than usual*. I have learned to monitor this tendency by watching how I use the air-conditioning system in my car. For example, I know the problem is starting if on a cold day I reach for the cool-air button.

Emotionally I react to too much pressure by becoming *unrealistically optimistic*. If I allow this feeling to escalate, my bank balance and any staff I am working with suffer. I start to initiate projects which have very little chance of succeeding. I try to prevent this from happening by listening to justified criticism on work which I thought I had done well. If on reviewing it I can see that the work has not met my usual standard, I know that I am in need of some pressure management.

Behaviourally, when I am stressed *I become impossible to*

live with. I am cued to this nowadays by my children. Instead of retorting back when they say something like, 'Oh, go to bed Daddy, you're grumpy tonight', I go up to my room, light some candles and either have a bath, meditate or go to sleep.

> I UNDERSTAND THAT ONCE I HAVE REACHED
> MY MAXIMUM PERFORMANCE LEVELS,
> INCREASING PRESSURE CAN BE
> HARMFUL TO ME.

> I WILL LEARN MY EARLY WARNING SIGNALS
> IN REGARD TO MY BODILY FEELINGS, MY
> EMOTIONAL STATE, AND MY BEHAVIOUR.

Once you have identified your EWS it is very helpful to share them with other people in your life. This is because they may notice them before you do. Indeed, they may even have been inconvenienced by them; you may not notice that this is happening because you are so preoccupied and busy. Sometimes Gael does not notice the state of her desk until her office cleaner or her family point out the mess to her. Malcolm may not notice he has turned his air-conditioning down until his passengers complain that they are freezing!

If you do ask someone to help you monitor your EWS, make sure that it is understood by all parties that no excuses are allowed. When we are in a pressurized state we also become exceptionally good at finding apparently plausible reasons (other than our own poor pressure management) to explain why we are behaving or feeling the way we are. Moreover, we really do believe our rationalizations! We actually think that the freak weather, unusually low sales or strange virus, uncomfortable chair or spicy curry is to blame. So your friends and family may need some assertiveness training before they take on the task of helping you to monitor your EWS!

I WILL SEEK THE HELP OF OTHER PEOPLE
TO TELL ME WHEN THEY THINK I AM
EXPERIENCING MY PERSONAL WARNING
SIGNALS.

To help you identify your own EWS, we have compiled the following tables. Although these lists are by no means exhaustive (unrestrained, they could fill a book on their own!), we hope that they will give you a starting point. It may take you weeks, or even months, of self-monitoring and experimenting before you have identified all three signals. But usually people are able to pinpoint at least one within a few days.

Common Warning Signals
of the Onset of Stress

Behavioural

We (or more likely other people!) may notice the following signs in our behaviour:

- poor concentration
- inability to listen attentively
- talking too much
- inability to control giggling fits, nervous tics etc.
- talking too little – going quiet
- being reclusive e.g. always lunching alone
- increasing consumption of alcohol, nicotine etc.
- poor eating habits
- clock-watching
- rushing around
- inability to sort priorities
- shouting more than usual
- insensitivity to others' needs
- unpredictable outbursts of temper
- clumsiness
- untidiness or unkempt appearance
- nervous habits e.g. nail-biting, scratching, picking
- difficulty in making decisions
- poor planning leading to too tight schedules
- not completing tasks
- reluctance to delegate
- making 'mountains out of molehills'
- missed exercise workout or sport schedules
- not spending time on hobbies
- an empty social diary
- over protectiveness

- playing 'too safe' – not taking usual calculated risks
- over spending and mounting debt
- getting up or going to bed too late

- sleep disturbance (early waking and insomnia or nightmares)
- forgetfulness (e.g. missed appointments, birthdays)
- losing control over finances

Emotional

Depending on our individual personality and the social and cultural factors affecting us, we may feel one or more of the following:

- irritable
- over-anxious
- restless
- uncontrollably worried
- moody
- overexcited
- pessimistic
- humourless
- continually guilty
- confused
- overwhelmed
- out of control
- powerless
- a decrease in confidence

- an increase in obsessions or phobias
- easily hurt or upset
- tearful
- worthless
- a lack of excitability or passion
- apathetic
- mistrustful of people – increased cynicism
- isolated
- depersonalised attachment (a feeling of watching the world from the outside)

Physical

- stomach cramps
- tension headaches
- tight scalp
- tired eyes
- blocked sinuses
- humming in the ears
- dry mouth
- sweating
- bowel problems – diarrhoea or constipation
- frequent urination
- muscle fatigue

- hunched posture
- stiffness in joints
- shoulder, back or neck ache
- skin rashes
- frequent 'pins and needles'
- cold hands and feet
- dizziness
- excessive PMS or disturbed menstrual cycle
- loss of libido or impotence
- frequent viral infections

Finally, it is important to remember that your EWS may need to change as you, your body and your life change. So every year or so it is a good idea to stop and check whether they are still the same for you.

I WILL CONTINUALLY UPDATE MY PERSONAL
EARLY WARNING SIGNALS AS I BECOME
MORE AWARE OF MY RESPONSE TO
PRESSURE.

STRESS-BEATERS: 'THE SIX Rs'

In this section we will introduce you to a range of strategies and techniques which we ourselves find useful and have proved to be favourites on our courses. We have arranged them in six sections and given each a title which begins with R, to make them easy to remember:

1 Relax
2 Review
3 Refuse
4 Resource
5 Reframe
6 Renew

We suggest that you learn this list off by heart. You can then use it as checklist to work through when your Early Warning Signals (see page 63) have alerted you to the fact that you have reached the top of your pressure curve.

As you read through these next sections you may find that in some areas you are already very knowledgeable and competent; in others you are less so. We suggest that you skim-read through everything at least once. Reading about what we already know in other people's words helps to fix it more firmly in our brains. (And who couldn't benefit from a gentle reminder or two when it comes to pressure management?!)

We hope you will find enough ideas to be able design your own individual *Positive Under Pressure* management tool-kit. But of course, our list of strategies is far from exhaustive. They are probably just the tip of the iceberg of pressure-management tools that could help you. So if our suggestions don't work for you, please trust that there will be others that can achieve the same effect. You will find many other ideas in the books in our Further Reading chapter. The important point to remember is that your individual pressure-management programme should include at least one strategy or exercise to cover each of the six Rs.

> THE MORE INDIVIDUALLY TAILORED MY
> *POSITIVE UNDER PRESSURE* PROGRAMME,
> THE MORE LIKELY IT IS TO BE
> SUCCESSFUL.

It may help to think of your first reading of our six Rs as a kind of 'window shopping'. During your second reading, take as much time as you can to 'try the material on for size and comfort'. You may then want to adapt and alter the strategies until they work best for you.

Your final task will be to design your own programme. We suggest that you then write this out, using our 6R headings as a guide. At the end of the book there is a 'shopping list' which you can use for this purpose. You could also use it to jot down notes as you are reading.

1

RELAX

Relaxation is a word which is used very freely in our society. It may have very different meanings for different people. In the context of our *Positive Under Pressure* programme it has a very specific meaning: It is used to describe the kind of activities which reverse the physiological disturbances associated with stress. Many other activities which are commonly called 'relaxing' – however pleasant they may be – do not necessarily achieve this particular end. When people in our groups are asked what they do to help themselves relax, they immediately reply by listing activities such as gardening, swimming, walking the dog, going for a run. Alternatively, they may list less active pursuits such as reading a book or listening to music. Although these are undoubtedly helpful, they do not have the same power to change the physiological effects of stress on our bodies or clear our minds as the techniques which we will be introducing to you in this chapter.

The scientific literature on the positive benefits of the kind of relaxation techniques we advocate is almost as definitive as the benefits of an operation for appendicitis, or antibiotics for pneumonia. The most successful of all have proved to be those which combine physiological reversal and mind clearing, such as meditation.

What Happens in Our Bodies When We Truly Relax?

It has been known for a long time that during the stress reaction the muscles become far more tense than usual. Pure physical/neuromuscular relaxation helps to reverse this tension. At the same time, our heart rate and blood pressure come down, and our breathing slows down. Some techniques such as meditation will also decrease our oxygen consumption and alter the pattern of our brain waves – but in such a way that our mental alertness is not impaired. This means that we need less oxygen in the body and therefore we breathe more slowly and can stay more calm. Pure relaxation takes the brainwave on the path towards sleep, whereas meditation does not do this.

We also know that relaxation decreases the production of adrenaline, nor-adrenaline and cholesterol.

Relaxation has also been shown to help treat some of the illnesses which are associated with chronic stress. In 60 per cent of studies where psychological and cognitive changes have been measured, it has been shown that anxiety levels – as well as a number of symptomatic complaints such as nervousness, sleeping difficulties, headaches and shortness of breath – can be reduced using relaxation techniques. In a recent review of mind/body therapies in the treatment of cardio-vascular disease, carried out by Stanford University in California, techniques such as these were found to be very effective. Other studies have also indicated that relaxation can have a beneficial effect on chronic pain, ulcerative colitis, rheumatoid arthritis, headaches, asthma and the pain of cancer.

Relaxation can also help people to overcome and control some chronic mental illnesses. For example, it is a proven treatment for panic disorders and anxiety. These techniques are now also widely taught to people who experience regular bouts of depression.

In addition, relaxation can help us in our everyday lives by boosting our ability to use our potential. It is now widely known that top sports performers use many of these techniques, particularly visualization. A survey of New Zealand rowers showed that 7 per cent used meditation, 64 per cent used relaxation and 61 per cent used visualization. These athletes found benefit from them all. Similarly, successful figure skaters use relaxation and positive thinking, and wrestlers, golfers and tennis and basketball players have found visualization to be very effective. (Basketball star Magic Johnson would not be half as magic without them!) This kind of success has convinced many trainers in the world of business, who are now teaching these techniques to 'corporate athletes'.

We are often asked which is more useful to relieve stress: thinking techniques or relaxation techniques. The answer, of course, is that you have to do both. In surveys of stress-management programmes, relaxation techniques have been shown to be more effective for reducing the physiological and biochemical changes of stress, while cognitive behavioural therapy is more suited to altering negative thinking. There is certainly no doubt in our minds, after considering the research and survey data as well as our own practical experience, that using a combination of techniques will substantially reduce most mental and physical stress symptoms.

Total Relaxation

We find that most people we meet rarely fully relax their whole body. A substantial number cannot remember ever having experienced the feeling. (They almost certainly did so when they were still babes in their mother's arms, but maybe that was the last time that they did!) So, if you are like them, you may need to practise the exercises repeatedly over several weeks before you can expect to experience deep relaxation or a meditative state.

When you first begin to relax in this way, it can feel alien and sometimes scary. It can seem as though you are losing control and drifting into a vulnerable state. (This is why so many people cannot be hypnotized.) The reality is that, although you may feel distanced from the world around you and disconnected from your body during this type of relaxation, you are not. You are conscious and can still exert self-control. And, even though it is much more pleasant to leave this state gradually, you can snap yourself out of it very quickly and easily if you need to do so.

So, as it may take some time for you to feel comfortable about entering this state, we suggest that initially you start by staying there for just a minute or two. Even after this short amount of time you should notice some benefit. You can then gradually increase your relaxation regime until you can stay in the state for 20 minutes. The good news is that the more experienced you become at relaxing, the less time it will take you to reach the most beneficial state. So if initially it takes you half an hour to achieve this, after practice you may be able to get there in less than a minute. A further bit of good news is that if you regularly practise relaxation, you will never again need to spend as much time calming your system down. We find that in our normal everyday busy lives, five minutes of relaxation two to three times a day can keep us free of tension. When we know that the pressure will be extraordinary, we may need to programme in slightly longer periods.

The secret undoubtedly lies in giving yourself small regular doses so that there is never a build-up of tension. When tension becomes chronically installed in our bodies it can be almost impossible to shift without a long, time-consuming period away from all pressure.

A final piece of encouragement to the devotees of cat-napping among you. A few moments of deep relaxation is much more physically and mentally re-vitalizing than a few hours of snatched sleep. This is especially true if you're the type of person who tends to nod off in uncomfortable positions with your worries still churning in your mind, waking to find you have missed more of the day than you wanted to!

In our *Positive Under Pressure* seminars we break relaxation training down into a number of stages, focusing on five:

1 posture
2 breathing
3 active neuromuscular relaxation for the body
4 sensory relaxation techniques for the body
5 meditation for the mind.

Once you have mastered the basics in each area, you can mix and match the techniques to suit yourself and your circumstances. The ones we will introduce you to are those which we ourselves now use most frequently, but we recognize that they may not turn out to be your favourites. We have listed a number of books in the Further Reading chapter which you can use to help. So there's really no excuse!

We suggest that you practise posture and breathing every morning and every evening for at least a week, then gradually introduce one of the other more complete relaxation techniques.

Remember, relaxation training is just like training your body at the gym. To gain the full benefit *you have to do it more than you want, for longer than you want, and more repetitively than you want!*

Before we start some practice, let's consider what kind of environment is most conducive to relaxation.

Where to Relax

Although you should eventually reach the stage of being able to achieve a relaxed state wherever you are, there are undoubtedly some environments which are more conducive than others. When you are first learning the exercises you will find it very helpful to create a special place. If you use it frequently, its 'pattern' of colours, sounds, shapes and smells will become embedded in the architecture of your brain and become neurologically associated with the state of relaxation. This means that you can fast-track yourself to a state of inner calm whenever you need to. This is important because, unfortunately, most people's lives do not include the ability to hop on to a jet and retreat to a desert island whenever they feel the need!

With a little preparation and minimal expenditure you can create a haven which can be very effective for relaxation purposes. And if you really *want* (rather than *need*) to head for that desert island, we are sure you can think of plenty of other good excuses for doing so!

Perhaps the ideal 'everyday' environment for relaxation is a room which is sound-proofed and lockable. It should also be one which can be easily darkened and lit with a few candles. Our brains are programmed to switch our bodies into low energy mode during the night; they do this by producing the hormone melatonin which helps us to sleep. As you don't want to sleep but merely to relax, it is advisable to have some form of gentle light on. If the room cannot be darkened, you can use a light blindfold (that is, one which dims rather than blocks out all light – a light blue or grey muslin scarf would work well).

If you are someone who finds music relaxing, your room should obviously have a CD or tape player. Be careful, however, to choose the right kind of music – this should be more 'bland' than lively or interesting and have a steady rhythm. It should not distract your attention from your relaxation exercises when you are first learning your techniques. At first, try to use the same kind of music over and over again to encourage your brain to establish a neurological link between the music and the state of relaxation.

As an alternative to music you could use some form of gentle rhythmic sound. Many people now install a small indoor fountain in the room which they use regularly for this purpose. Alternatively you could play specially recorded relaxation CDs or tapes featuring sounds of the forest or the sea, or bird song or dolphins.

The colours and furniture of the room are not so important, as the room will be fairly dark. But if you are re-decorating, bear in mind that blues, greens and lavender are known to be calming. If you are buying new furniture you may want to look for soft curves rather than angular shapes.

You could also burn some aromatherapy oils such as lavender or sandalwood, or some incense. We have recommended several books on this subject in the Further Reading chapter, so that you can be sure to use the correct oil/incense for you. Don't forget, however pleasant they may be, many aromas enliven rather than relax, and some are not recommended if you are pregnant or are suffering from certain medical conditions.

Now, having whetted your appetite for this perfect location, let's return to reality! First, you may not have a spare room which you can set aside for relaxation. If you don't, you could use the bathroom or create a special relaxation area somewhere which you could even corner off with a screen. You could keep a box of relaxation 'tools' there such as a personal stereo with your CDs or tapes, your light blindfold and aromatherapy burner.

So, especially while you are learning these skills, make it easy on yourself and go to your prepared relaxation room as often as you can. Don't forget that when you cannot be there in reality, you can use your mind's eye to take you there. Through using your imaginative powers to recall its colours, shapes, sounds and aromas, you will be able to summon up a sense of peace and calm instantly, wherever you may happen to be.

Posture

Good posture is an essential pre-condition for relaxation. If you need convincing, just spend some time observing the most chronically tense worrier you know. You'll probably notice that they hold their body in a tight 'hunch' most of the time. Their head will be bowed forward, their shoulders rounded, and every limb and finger will be held in a tightly crossed or clenched position. If we happen to have just described your posture for much of the time, you may need to get some professional help and advice before you will feel the benefit of the exercises we will be introducing. We would suggest that, as soon as possible, you consult a qualified (and personally recommended, if possible) practitioner such as a:

physiotherapist
osteopath
Alexander Technique teacher
yoga teacher
fitness trainer.

Any one of these will be able to advise you on how to change and maintain your posture so that you do not habitually create unnecessary tension in your body. Most of these practitioners will also be able to manipulate you physically to relieve the effects of accumulated chronic tension. Alternatively, they may instruct you in a programme of exercises which will achieve the same outcome.

Once your chronic tension has been relieved, don't be tempted to postpone your relaxation training. The best time to learn it is when you need it least. You will achieve the optimum relaxed state so much more quickly and you will be much more motivated to develop the habit of taking yourself there on a regular basis.

It is important to be able to practise relaxation in a variety of postures. This will enable you to release your tension whether you are standing outside an interview room, sitting in a crowded train or lying on a beach in the Bahamas.

These guidelines may sound a bit too much like common sense to some of you, but our experience has shown that most people need them.

Standing

- Put both your feet firmly on the ground and slightly apart. Press your heels, soles and toes downwards as far as possible to get full support for as much of the surface area of your feet as possible.
- Shrug your shoulders several times and then relax them into

a comfortable position, checking that they are not rounding forward.

- Unclench and unwind all your limbs, allowing your hands to rest by your sides or gently supported in your pockets.
- Push your chin slightly forward until your eyes are looking out in a direct horizontal line.
- Imagine that you have a strong fine thread running through your spine and that it is being continuously pulled up through your head in a straight vertical line, to help you maintain an upright posture.

Sitting

- If you can, choose a chair with a straight back and a head support.
- Uncross your legs and place them firmly on the ground as above. Put your knees in a position so that your legs are held at an angle of 90 degrees.
- Uncross your arms and hands and lay them loosely on your thighs. Alternatively, some people like to put their hands in the position of Christian prayer with the palms flat against each other. This is thought to be a very stabilizing position, and immediately conveys a non-verbal message to your brain and to others that you are in control of yourself. Other people like to place their hands in the position of Buddhist meditation – their thumbs and index fingers lightly touching, forming an 'O'.
- Drop your shoulders and push gently back until they feel loose, straight and in balance.
- Sit well back in the chair so that your weight is being supported by your buttocks and there is little pressure on your coccyx at the base of your spine. Imagine, as above, a thin wire running through your spine gently pulling your back, neck and head into a straight upright position. If you have a head rest you may need to adjust it to find the most supportive position. When travelling, even for short distances,

try to remember to take inflatable neck and back support
pillows. These (together with your eye-mask and earplugs)
will enable you to convert the most uncomfortable seating
into your relaxing haven!

- Take a few moments to feel the support of the chair's back
  and seat and the firmness of the ground beneath your feet.
  You should be able to imagine your body melting into these
  surfaces. Some people also find it helpful to imagine that
  they are drawing up a supply of the energy which is deeply
  embedded in the earth and has accumulated over the
  billions of years of existence.

Sitting on the Floor

- Sit crossed-legged on the floor.
- Relax your shoulders.
- Ensure that your back and neck are as straight and leng-
  thened as possible.
- Rest your hands in one of the positions described above, or
  face upwards with palms open on your knees.

Lying Down

- Choose a flat softened surface such as a thick rug or exercise mat or a firm mattress.
- Ensure that your body is straight and pressed evenly against
  the floor.
- Support your neck if it is tense with a neck pillow or small
  rolled towel.
- Support the arch of your back with a rolled towel if you
  have a large space between the arch of your back and the
  floor and do not feel comfortable.
- Relax your hands and lay them on either side of you, preferably with palms facing upwards.

Breathing

Once you have your posture right it is time to concentrate on the pattern, regularity, depth and speed of your breathing. Most people find this easiest to do with their eyes shut, although we occasionally meet people who prefer to have their eyes open.

There are two important points to remember when you are doing breathing exercises. The first is that you must make your breathing slower, deeper and more regular than usual. The second is that you should concentrate on the process, using your imagination to help you to follow the flow of air as it passes through your body.

During your breathing exercises you will need to consciously push your diaphragm down. This is the muscle between your stomach and your chest, just under your ribs. You should feel your stomach pushing out. This may feel slightly strange as it is not most people's normal pattern of breathing, but it does allow you to take a much deeper breath. When you breathe out, do the reverse. Bring your diaphragm up and your stomach in.

Do this simple exercise now before reading any further:

❸XERCISE

While keeping your focus on the passage of your breath through your body:

- Slowly breathe in through your nose, expanding your lungs as fully as you can, pushing your diaphragm down and your stomach out.
- Hold your breath for five to ten seconds.
- Exhale slowly through your nose while lifting your diaphragm and bringing your stomach in.
- Repeat several times, each time taking slightly longer to complete the cycle and trying to keep the passage of air flowing at a steady, even rate.

This kind of breathing will immediately slow your heart rate and bring your blood pressure down.

The following additional techniques may help you to do this exercise even more effectively. Use or adapt them as part of your individual relaxation programme.

Colour Breathing

As you take a breath in, imagine that you are inhaling white energy. On your out-breath, imagine that you are exhaling breath that is coloured orange. Every time a thought comes into your mind, return the focus of your attention to these colours.

Meditating on the Quality of Your Breath

As you breathe in, focus your attention on the character of the air as it passes through your body. Does it feel cooler than normal? Is it fresher than normal? Can you smell the incense or the freshness of the air? Is it stimulating and invigorating? Similarly, when you breathe out try to notice how the character of the air has changed. Is it warmer? Has the smell gone? Is the smell different? Is it less fresh?

Breathing with a Mantra

As you breathe, say one or two words. Some people just say 'in' and 'out' as they breathe, others may choose to say a word such as 'one', 'energy', 'strength'. If you have been taught transcendental meditation or meditation associated with a religion or sect, you may have been taught a particular mantra. One that Malcolm uses is 'Om, Namah, Shivaya', which comes from the practice of Sidha yoga. 'Om' is the universal first sound of creation, and as such is, according to Sidha yoga teachers, able to bring the strength of the previous eternities. 'Namah' means worship or respect, and 'Shivaya' your own inner strength, inner being, inner wholeness or inner god.

Energy Breathing

As you breathe in, imagine you are inhaling fresh revitalizing energy. When you exhale, imagine that you are breathing out your stress and tension.

Active Neuromuscular Relaxation

Once your posture and breathing are right, you can begin to relax your body.

Active neuromuscular relaxation is achieved by first contracting and then relaxing each of the major muscle groups in turn. This allows you to feel the difference between contraction (tension) and relaxation. The idea is that, in the end, you will be able to relax your muscles without going through the contracting phase, as you will know what the difference feels like. However, this may take some time.

When Malcolm teaches this exercise he starts with the muscles in the top of the head, working down to those in the tips of the toes. He finds this better than going the other way, as it is then possible, at the same time, to visualize all the tension slowly washing out of your body and into the ground below you. He finds that the reverse procedure seems to trap the tension in the head as you slowly relax upwards. Gael, on the other hand, finds starting with the feet works for her, possibly because this was how she was taught to do it many years ago and her brain is familiar with this order. In this exercise we are going to work from the head downwards. Try doing it this way several times, but if it doesn't work, reverse the order in which you relax the muscles.

Remember while you are doing the exercise to keep your breathing deep, slow and regular, and maintain a good posture. (It may help, until you are completely familiar with this sequence, to tape-record it and play it back to yourself as a guide, so you can concentrate primarily on your breathing.)

Facial Muscles

- Lift your eyebrows upwards as high as they will go, as you try to tense your scalp muscles, and then relax them.
- Close your eyes tight, as tight as you possibly can. Feel all the tension, and then relax them.
- Curl your upper lip up to your nose. Feel the tension, then relax.
- Do the same with your lower lip.
- Curl up your tongue in your mouth, clench your teeth, then relax.
- Move your jaw forwards and backwards.

At this stage, stop concentrating on your breathing and feel how relaxed your head is feeling.

Upper Body Muscles

- Bend your chin forward to touch your chest. Feel the tension, then relax. Push your head gently backwards – as far back as it will go. Feel the tension, then relax. Turn your head slowly to the left. Feel the tension, then relax. Turn your head to the right. Feel the tension. Relax.
- Shrug your shoulders as high up as they will go. Feel the tension. Relax. Push your shoulder blades back. Feel the tension. Relax. Bring your shoulders forward. Feel the tension. Relax.

Upper Limbs

- Press your arms into your sides, as tight as you can. Relax. Bend your arms at the elbows. Squeeze as tight as you can. Relax.
- Curl your knees up (one at a time if you are standing) to try to touch your chest. Relax.
- Bend your wrists backwards as far as they will go. Relax.
- Clench your hands as tight as you can. Relax.

Now return your attention to your breathing. Check that you are breathing deeply and slowly.

Stomach and Pelvic Muscles

- Pull your stomach in as tight as you can. Relax.
- Contract your anal muscles and your pelvic floor as tight as you can. Relax.

Now concentrate on your breathing again.

Lower Limbs

- Bring your left knee to your chest as tight as you can. Relax.
- Bring your right knee to your chest as tight as you can. Relax.
- With bent knees, press both knees together as tight as you can. Relax.
- Bend each heel backwards as far as you can. Relax.
- Stretch each foot forward as tight as you can. Relax.
- Curl your toes up as tight as you can. Relax.

Go back to your breathing.

By this time you will have learned the difference between tension and relaxation in all your major muscle groups.

Sensory Relaxation Techniques

The following exercises, or variations on the exercises above, involve using one of your senses. Doing this usually speeds up relaxation because the senses have such direct links with our emotional brain centres.

- As you slowly contract the muscle groups, visualize the tension being pushed out of your body from the top downwards and out of your feet.
- Once you have got your body into a very relaxed state,

imagine your favourite coloured light circling just above
your head, and allow your imagination to take this light
through each of the muscle groups we have previously
described. Take it slowly, first through the head, neck,
upper body, shoulders and chest, then the stomach, pelvic
floor, legs and feet. As you visualize the coloured light travelling through your body, imagine its heat and vibration helping you to relax. Do this two or three times and imagine
that you are bathed in your favourite light and your favourite degree of warmth. After two to four weeks of practice
you may be able to get yourself into a relaxed state just by
visualizing the light going through your body, and will no
longer have to do the active contracting and relaxing.

Scenic Tour Visualization

Choose a scene which has peaceful memories for you. You are
going to take yourself on an imaginary tour of your scene. As
you breathe in, take your mind's eye from the beginning to the
midway point of your 'tour'; use your out-breath to finish your
'tour'.

This is Gael's favourite relaxation technique. She uses the view
from the back of her house in Spain. As she has been using it
for many years, usually her brain instantly switches into relaxed
mode at the first sight of the fountain in her imagination. If she
is particularly stressed or worried she may need to do a couple
of 'tours' to achieve total relaxation.

Comfort Zone Visualization

Take your mind to the most comforting place you can remember
or imagine. To some people this means being curled up on their
sides in the foetal position in bed, or for others even within their
mother's womb. Some people imagine being bathed in water and
warmth at the same time. Others imagine that they are tucked
up in bed on a cold night with their own warmth under the

blankets, or are sitting in front of a roaring fire in a country cottage. Malcolm imagines that he is sitting in a shady glen in the Welsh mountains beside a babbling brook, with a little waterfall, new-cut grass, flowers, butterflies and twittering birds in the sunlight.

Use your senses to bring your scene into sharp focus in your imagination. Recreate in your mind its sounds, smells, colours, movement and the feeling of your skin.

Anchoring a Positive Feeling

Anchoring is a technique which enables us to utilize past experiences of relaxation to help us instantly access the same positive state of feeling. (Often referred to as a 'resource state'.) It involves encouraging our brain, through a visualization process, to make a neural association between the feeling response of our past experience and a particular word, sound or small movement. When you have learned the technique you will be able to adapt it for anchoring other useful resource states such as a feeling of confidence or optimism. Programming the brain to associate the positive feelings of a past experience with a particular thought, word, or physical sensation or movement enables us to recall the positive emotional feelings whenever we say the word or sound, or make the associated physical movement.

In a deeply relaxed (but still conscious!) state, recall, in as much vivid detail as possible, an experience from the past which helped you to feel calm and at peace. Use your imagination to 're-live' the experience physically and emotionally. Recall the experience of your senses. See the colours, shapes and positive facial expressions. Hear all the sounds of the scene. Imagine yourself touching some of the objects in the scene and feel the various textures.

Spend a few minutes enjoying the feelings that accompanied this experience. Notice what was happening (or not happening!) in your body. Now heighten the feeling and make yourself sense it as deeply as you can. While holding on to the feeling, say a particular word and/or make a small discreet movement (for example, touching a part of your body or moving a limb in a certain kind of way). The movement should be one that you will be able to do later in public without anyone noticing.

Repeat the above steps several times before bringing yourself gently back into the real world.

Repeat the whole anchoring exercise as many times as you can over the next few weeks. You will know when you have successfully anchored your resource state in your brain when you can do your movement and say your word and find that you are feeling more calm as a result.

Experiment, as soon as you can, with using your anchor in real-life situations. The more often you use the anchor, the more powerful and useful it will be.

Make a note on a card of the following stages in the anchoring process, so you can practise it whenever you have a spare few moments:

- relax
- recall
- re-live
- anchor
- repeat.

Depending on how easy it is for you to take yourself into a deeply relaxed state, it could take from 8 – 12 weeks to master all these stages of the anchoring process. Remember, do them slowly and carefully. Experiment until you find what is the best kind of anchor for you.

⊖XERCISE

Think of a scene which you could use to anchor a positive state of calm in your brain. Make some short notes which you can use when you next do your anchoring practice.

The event was:

I was wearing:

These were the smells which I recall:

These were the colours:

These people were present:

These were their facial expressions:

The weather was:

Add any other notes on the scene which would help your visualization:

I WILL RELAX MY BODY THOROUGHLY
ONCE EVERY DAY.

Meditation

Meditation is often regarded as a spiritual exercise. This is because it has been used for centuries by both Eastern and Western religions as a means of attaining a special state of consciousness which is associated with mystic experience and an ascetic holy life. Although some of you may also want to use it for this purpose, our interest in it now is purely for its use as a tool to help clear our minds so we can relax more deeply. Meditation also stimulates our creativity.

There are literally hundreds of different meditation techniques. They all share one common trait: they help us to close off the outside world and cocoon ourselves mentally in an inner chamber of our mind. They enable us to switch out of rational thinking mode and allow our mind to go into a very relaxed 'free-floating' state. This is achieved by fully concentrating our attention on one thing and one thing only. This could, for example, be a candle flame, a flower, a word, a repetitive sound, a body sensation or slow rhythmic exercise (as in some of the exercises above).

Alternatively you can focus your attention on a mandala, which is what we use when we first introduce the technique on our courses. A mandala is a balanced geometric pattern (often quite intricate and beautiful) which draws your eye to a central point. Mandalas have been used for centuries by many different religions and are often built into churches or other places of worship where people meditate. Some famous cathedrals such as York Minster in England and Notre Dame in Paris have very beautiful mandalas in their main stained glass windows. In many traditional Islamic and Southern Spanish buildings you will find tiles with a variety of mandala patterns.

The reason we choose to work with mandalas is that they make the first stage of meditation very easy. In order to perceive the mandala's pattern, our brains automatically switch out of left-brain (rational) mode and into right-brain (spatial) mode. This means that our mind, without any conscious prodding from us, immediately stops chewing over problems and worries.

Opposite is an example of a design we ourselves use for meditation.

A Mandala Meditation

First adopt one of your relaxed postures. Then take a few deep slow breaths and just focus your attention on the central point of the design. The moment you notice your attention wandering, gently bring it back to the central point.

Soon your mind will start to 'float' as your eyes begin (of their own accord) to wander out to the sides of the design and then back again to the centre. If you continue to focus on your mandala for five minutes or so you should experience a feeling of lightness in your body as you drift into a deeply relaxed state.

When you stop looking at the mandala and bring yourself back

into the world, your mind will feel once again clear and energetic.
You may even have forgotten what you were worrying about!
Indeed, when you do remember, you may well find you have a
new idea about how to solve the problem which was obsessing
your mind. This is because the mandala meditative process also
stimulates the part of our brain where our creative thinking
'muscles' are housed. So this kind of meditation rewards you
with two 'pay-offs' for the price of one!

Why not try it for yourself NOW? You can use our illustration
for the moment, but we suggest that later you find a colourful
mandala that is appealing to your own individual eye. You can
find them very easily in New Age or religious shops where they
are often sold as cards. Alternatively, you could always dig out
your old school compass and draw and colour one for yourself!

As we said earlier, you may have to persist for several weeks
or even months with these exercises before you will begin to
experience deep relaxation. But in the meantime you should feel
some benefits. They will certainly help you to feel calmer than

you were before you used them. At first you may find yourself being distracted by outside noises such as children shouting, a car horn hooting or an aeroplane flying overhead. If this happens, try imagining that all these extraneous sounds are like clouds in the sky, drifting gently in and out of your consciousness. Then before proceeding with the relaxation, gently return your attention to your breathing for a moment or two.

I WILL RELAX AND CLEAR MY MIND WITH
MEDITATION AT LEAST ONCE A DAY.

2

REVIEW

After practising all those relaxation exercises in the last chapter, can we assume that you are now bouncing with mental and physical energy? If so, perhaps the pressures in your life no longer look so overwhelming, and you are becoming confident that you can return to the fray without doing anything else. We know this pattern so well. We understand the temptation. It is hard to set aside even more time to dwell on your problems when they are *feeling* more manageable and when there are so many others needing your attention.

The reality is that your good feeling will quickly pass if you return to your pressures without reviewing your lifestyle and behaviour. This is, of course, especially true if your Early Warning Signals were ringing their bells before you started your relaxation schedule.

Perhaps Peter's story will illustrate this for us.

Peter is a manager of a large theatre. It is a job he loves. He always wanted to work in this world and knows that the job is ideally suited to his strengths and skills. He has until the last year been very successful. Now he's bending badly under the pressure.

One of his external problems is that, increasingly over the last few years, he has been spending a disproportionate amount of time taking calls from irate customers. They are angry because they have been trying to contact the theatre for hours and have only just managed to get through. They are often personally abusive, and several have made threats to report the theatre to the Arts Council for poor service. Peter feels frustrated because he has been asking the owners for a new telephone system for five years. He is further frustrated when he is told that box office numbers are down and that they need to make further cuts, not increase their expenditure.

Peter spends so much time placating customers and the owners that he has to stay at work for an extra two hours every night. This lifestyle is putting a strain on his marriage. In a recent row, in front of his son Joe, his wife told him that he has only read Joe a bedtime story once in the last three months. He knows he is not being the kind of father he had hoped to be.

He is finding that he is becoming more and more anxious and indecisive when doing even the most menial parts of his job. Sometimes he finds himself sitting staring into space because he doesn't know what to do next. Then his mind starts its worrying merry-go-round. These are the kind of questions and thoughts which circulate around and around in his head:

'Should I stand up to the abuse from customers? But I can't afford to lose any. Should I contact the Arts Council myself? But I can't afford to alienate the management. Should I agree to a trial separation from my wife? But I still love her. Should I stop working overtime and give my son priority? I might lose my job and then he would suffer even more. Should I give up this dream job and go back to teaching? But I was stressed by that job too. Should I get a job in the business world and make loads of money and retire early? But I'd hate that kind of life. Should I see my doctor and get some Prozac? But then that would be registered in my medical records. Should I now finish my monthly report or check the safety curtain, or ring back John or check the ice cream order has gone through or go to the first rehearsal or go to the printers? But they've all got to be done today and I can't do them all. I might as well have another coffee and toss a coin.'

When Peter began to feel like this six months ago, he took himself for a short break. After a few days of walking alone in the hills and fishing in peaceful streams, he felt calmer and more in control. On his return to work, however, his feelings and indecisiveness quickly returned.

Once a confident, outgoing, successful manager, Peter is now reduced to being an inefficient and unassertive ditherer. Understandably, Peter feels his internal and external pressures are becoming totally intolerable. He has begun to take a fatalistic attitude – he is convinced that a crisis is imminent. He even takes comfort in this thought because then it will be someone else who'll have to make the decisions and take the 'flack'. He has started to seriously daydream about 'chucking it all in' and becoming a sheep farmer in some isolated terrain far removed from the buzz of the busy life he really loves.

Hopefully you are not in this kind of extreme situation and never have been. But even so, you may be able to identify with some aspects of Peter's underlying problems. Under pressure, haven't you sometimes:

found that you have lost sight of what your main priorities in
     life are?
lost faith in your ability to judge what is the right thing to do?
started abdicating your personal power and letting other
     people or 'Fate' or fantasy take over the direction of your
     life?

We believe that Peter and anyone else who has similar symptoms needs to 'get back to basics' before he takes any other action. Before he can regain control of his life, he needs to review the core principles by which he (and no other) wants to lead it. First he needs to *anchor* himself with a few simple rules to give him a sense of personal security and enable him to make some decisions. We are sure that, earlier in his career, he would have had these rules perhaps without having realized it. The reason why he had been able to handle dilemmas and difficult choices was partly due to the fact that he had a clear idea of what his basic guiding values and priorities were. But over the years his own personal circumstances and the environment in which he is working changed, and he must now reassess and update these rules.

With hindsight, Peter can see that when he noticed his Early Warning Signals he should have taken time out not just to relax and regain control of his physical stress, but for some serious review.

Ideally, we would hope that one day Peter will see Review not merely as something to be done when there are signs of trouble in the pressure camp. We believe that anyone who takes on the extra responsibilities of living life in the fast lane needs to monitor their progress much more regularly and thoroughly than other people with less pressure.

As we have said earlier, the path to stress is a slippery slope and one which is extremely easy to glide down very gradually and unknowingly. If we want to stay in the business of prevention, we must continually remind ourselves (and each other!) that the best time to do this kind of work is when we appear to need it least.

The eventual outcome we would like you to achieve is to make Review, in some manageable form, part of your everyday behaviour. We would like it to become a constant habit that you can take for granted. But, having said that, this is a standard we know that we ourselves have never reached. We still find it hard to set aside precious time for introspection when there is no particular crisis kicking us into that mode. This is why we prefer to ensure that regular times for Review are structured into our agenda.

The depth of Review you will need and the amount of time you will require to do it efficiently will vary tremendously. But there are three main tasks which we suggest you can benefit from doing from time to time:

1 Assess your current level of pressure.
2 Re-examine your personal standards and life rules.
3 Reassess your needs and priorities.

Assess Your Current Level of Pressure

We've devised the following checklist to help you do this task on a monthly basis. When you have completed the questionnaire you will have a clearer idea of how much time and attention you may need to give to the rest of your Review. (It may even indicate, for a lucky few, that they can skip the rest of this chapter with a clear conscience!)

My Current Pressure and Stress Levels
Scoring

1 Never
2 Occasionally
3 Frequently
4 Consistently

I do not meet my own expectations of myself.	1	2	3	4
I am unable to ask for things I need.	1	2	3	4
I cannot tell people when I am overworked or do not know the answer.	1	2	3	4
My desk is in a mess.	1	2	3	4
I have unpaid bills.	1	2	3	4
I cannot delegate tasks.	1	2	3	4
I am getting palpitations, chest pain, or shortness of breath.	1	2	3	4
Things are going wrong, it is my own fault.	1	2	3	4
I find it difficult to concentrate.	1	2	3	4
I cannot cope with my current workload.	1	2	3	4

I am always tired.	1	2	3	4
People tell me I'm irritable.	1	2	3	4
I have a short fuse at present.	1	2	3	4
Little things make me anxious.	1	2	3	4
Nothing good is happening for me at the moment.	1	2	3	4
I never have enough time.	1	2	3	4
I am not sleeping well at present.	1	2	3	4
Small delays are frustrating me.	1	2	3	4
I take a long time to relax when I get home.	1	2	3	4
I do not have much patience at present.	1	2	3	4
I find it hard to complete tasks.	1	2	3	4
Decisions are difficult to make.	1	2	3	4
I have less energy than I would like.	1	2	3	4
I do not enjoy being with my friends.	1	2	3	4
My cigarette consumption has increased.	1	2	3	4
I am drinking more alcohol than I used to.	1	2	3	4
I can't work without drinking coffee, tea or coca cola.	1	2	3	4
I am using drugs both prescribed and illegal more than usual.	1	2	3	4
I am getting indigestion or heartburn.	1	2	3	4
My bowel habit has changed.	1	2	3	4
Headaches are now a problem.	1	2	3	4
Back ache stops me enjoying myself.	1	2	3	4
I never have time for lunch.	1	2	3	4
I cannot tell people how I feel about them.	1	2	3	4
People are always criticizing me.	1	2	3	4
I take on too much work.	1	2	3	4
I have less time for my hobbies than I used to.	1	2	3	4
I regret not saying 'No' more often.	1	2	3	4
I see the negative in most things.	1	2	3	4
I have too little resources to enjoy myself.	1	2	3	4

Results

40—75 Good control of stress – perhaps not enough pressure

76—94 Reasonable level – using pressure well to motivate

95—113 Stress level is getting high – watch your Early Warning Signals

114—160 Too much stress – time to decrease your pressure or
increase your resources (internal or external). You therefore
need to do some serious review!

> I COMMIT TO ASSESSING MY LEVEL OF
> PRESSURE AT LEAST ONCE A MONTH.

Re-examine Your Personal Standards and Life Rules

Why is it that most successful leading-edge businesses are now
investing large sums of money into clarifying company values
and working principles?

The short answer is that they are now convinced that it will
be good for business. They know that:

Their staff will be more confident, decisive and energized
because they have a clear idea of what is expected from
them and why they are doing what they are doing.

Team-work will improve because clear standards and principles bond a company together and help its people pull in
the same direction.

They will have fewer misunderstandings with the outside world
(including shareholders!) because others have a clearer idea
of what they can and cannot expect from the company.

It prevents many problems occurring because everyone has a
simple tool to help them check that they are on the right
track.

A welcome by-product of all this, of course, is that everyone (but
management in particular!) is under much less pressure!

We know that you can achieve very similar results for yourself
if you ensure that the way you run your own life remains in line
with your key values. Personal crises often force people into facing
this reality, as the following two stories illustrate. One person's
review led to an adjustment in his working schedule, the other

to a more major change. Both changes enabled these two people to live more comfortably with themselves because their lifestyle and behaviour were not in conflict with their personal standards. The results in both cases were that, although their lives are still very pressurized, they no longer suffer from stress and feel very much happier and more motivated.

Ian's Change of Schedule

Ian was a consultant in a management company who always arrived at work looking drained. He started to do a serious review of his life and his priorities when his daughter began having severe behavioural problems at school. One day at a family counselling session his daughter said, 'Daddy, you never have any time for me, I only wish you'd take me to school.'

This plea proved to be the key turning-point for Ian. He made the decision that on every day of her school life he would take Gloria to school, and after that he would go back home and have a coffee with his wife before going to work. He negotiated a new starting point for his day with his employers. He never arrived at work earlier than 10 a.m., but when he did come he looked fresh and happy and he worked in a much more motiv-ated way. Of course he had to compensate for his late start, and this often meant that he was writing up reports till as late as 11 p.m. at night. But he felt much happier and was working much more effectively because he had clarified his priorities and re-arranged his life so that he could honour these. His stress was immediately alleviated even though his pressures still remained enormous.

Melissa's Change of Career

Melissa was a successful doctor who had a very good general practice. She also had deeply religious beliefs and, like many doctors, was 100 per cent committed to her patients. Her enjoy-ment of being a doctor was enhanced by the fact that she believed she was doing God's work and that God acted through her to help get patients better.

Slowly but surely, she found that whenever she was treating physical illness she began thinking about the emotional and spiritual needs which she felt were contributing to the lack of well-being in her patients. The result was that a normal-five minute appointment for a cold could stretch to an hour. Her patients thrived on Melissa's holistic approach, but her own pressure began to escalate as the queues in the waiting room lengthened and her relationships (understandably) with her receptionists and other colleagues deteriorated.

After doing some serious reflecting, one day she suddenly realized that she had only become a doctor because her parents wanted her brother to be one and he had chosen to be a farmer. It was not her true 'calling'. She therefore took the very brave step of giving up general practice and returning to university to do a theology degree. She is now a very successful Methodist pastor, feeling much more fulfilled and satisfying a thriving congregation. But, reluctant to throw her medical skills completely away, she also spends half a day helping her local general practice out. She works just as hard but she now copes much better and enjoys her pressures.

Hopefully your life may not need such a thorough 'overhaul' as Melissa's did. Career changes can, after all, be very costly and very time-consuming. But maybe a little rescheduling of your agenda could make all the difference, as it did with Ian.

Take a moment to do the following exercise. It will give you an opportunity to check on whether your lifestyle is in tune with your values and principles.

Living by My Life Rules

- List 10 occasions when you felt most proud of yourself in the last year.

- List 10 examples of when you have let yourself down during the last year.
- Name your three most important Life Rules (that is, the principles by which you run your life and which influence most of your personal decision-making).

How easy did you find it to do this exercise?

Many people on our courses find it extremely difficult. Being intelligent, competent people, they cannot understand why such a simple task should prove so difficult. Occasionally we are told it is the exercise which is at fault – they say it is too simplistic!

We can relate to all these responses, but we ourselves have been amazed at how such a simple exercise can have had such a powerful impact on us and the way we manage our lives. Since we have clarified our own Life Rules, we have found our pressure almost magically reduced. Having these rules at the forefront of our conscious minds has helped us both to solve a number of serious dilemmas. But their main value has been that they have made our everyday decision-making so much easier. Of course we break our rules sometimes (you will have gathered that we are not saints!), but at least we know we are heading for trouble when we do.

We did not disclose our own personal Life Rules before giving you the exercise, because we wanted to ensure that you were not influenced by them. It is so easy when we are in a state similar to Peter's, Melissa's or Ian's to latch on to the 'wisdom' of 'gurus'. Stress tends to flip us back into a child-like state. It is natural to start looking around for 'parents' to guide us through our personal moral maze. But for Life Rules to work as a pressure-management tool they need to be unique to each individual.

So we will now share our own Life Rules, if only to prove that we have taken the medicine ourselves!

Malcolm's Current Three Rules

1 Always put my children first.
2 Never do anything that I would not wish to appear on the front page of *The News of the World*.
3 Treat other people as I would wish my granny to be treated.

This does not mean that Malcolm always does everything for his children and nothing for anybody else or himself. But when he does meet a clash of interests, he puts more weight on the benefit of his children, or his children's wishes. Of course, he also has to make judgements about whether his children truly need what they are asking for, and take into consideration what he believes they need in terms of time, money or practical help. So his children do not always get their own way, but their needs, wishes and wants do get a better hearing than anyone else's.

Malcolm's second rule does not guarantee that he will always lead a perfect life. But it does mean that he always considers the effect that his actions will have on others before he gives in to some of his urges. If he is tempted to stray from his own 'straight and narrow', he first asks himself if would wish his closest friends to read about his misdemeanours in the tabloid press.

Similarly, treating everyone as he would wish his granny to be treated does not mean that every old lady is helped across the road. But it has helped him to make more balanced judgements regarding the needs of other people. For example, if he would not mind his granny being left alone for a day, there is no reason why other people cannot do without his presence for half a day! Abiding by this rule has enabled him to obtain a better balance in his life.

Gael's Current Three Rules

1 Be true to myself and my values.
2 See the positive in change, however unwelcome it might seem.

3 Spend more time than I think I can afford on the relationships which matter most to me.

The first rule has helped Gael because when she begins to overload
herself with pressure, she loses some of her self-confidence. As
a result, she may be inclined to revert to her childhood habits
of living to please others rather than herself. So, by regularly
checking that what she is doing, saying or writing truly reflects
who she is today and what she really believes, she can stop herself
from taking on tasks which meet the needs of others at the
expense of her own self-respect.

Her second rule has a similar function. It is there to stop her
old negative inner demon from sabotaging her chances of seeing
the positive potential in change. This is a crucial rule because,
in fact, the 'true Gael' loves and thrives on change.

Gael's third rule has played a very important part in helping
her to keep her life in balance. Not only does it help her make
decisions about how much time she should allocate to her family
and close friends, it also helps her to ensure that she chooses to
work with people with whom she wants to work and makes an
effort to meet the kinds of people she would like to know. Now
whenever she feels disappointed that she hasn't the time, for
example, to meet her daughter while in London, take a phone
call from her husband at lunchtime, lead a course with a colleague
she likes or chat to a new interesting acquaintance, this rule pops
into her head as a timely warning.

We hope that you find your Life Rules become equally supportive. But don't forget that your rules should be making your life
easier to live. The moment that they start giving you pressure,
they should be reviewed again and changed.

I COMMIT TO LIVING BY MY OWN
PERSONAL RULES.

Reassess Your Needs and Priorities

Too much pressure undoubtedly distorts our perception. In extreme circumstances people can start believing that the very survival of the planet depends on them and them only. They also become convinced that they are totally indispensable to the people around them and that *everything* they need to do must be done NOW.

Do you recognize the pattern?

If you do, you are not alone because we do, and so do most people who come on our courses. The purpose of this part of your review is to check this tendency.

One of the mistakes we often find people make is that when they feel stressed they start hunting around for their old action plans and lists of priorities. They believe this will be the best and quickest way to 'get themselves back on track'. Unfortunately, this rarely works because either the circumstances or the people have changed, or the original objectives they had set themselves were unrealistic or inappropriate. However frustrating it may be in the short term to have to go back to the 'drawing board', we know that this is the only effective way to stop our pressure escalating beyond our control.

Start by doing this exercise, which should only take a few minutes.

⊜XERCISE

Make a list of needs you would like to meet during the *next week only*, under the following headings.

1 Work tasks
2 Family responsibilities
3 Self-esteem maintenance
4 Career/personal development
5 Health
6 Balanced life

Your next task will be to try and decide which of these tasks you have given yourself must be done *perfectly*, and which you can accept a *'good enough'* standard for. Our experience of working with people in this field is that it is overcrowded with perfectionists!

Taming Your Perfectionism

We are certainly not in the business of obliterating this wonderful personal quality. (Gael is especially fond of it!) It has undoubtedly contributed to the success of many great high achievers. Our aim is merely to ensure that it is under your control and not giving you unnecessary internal or external pressure.

Let's first remind ourselves of the dangers of allowing this character trait to run our lives.

Loneliness

Perfectionists are so busy they often do not have the time or energy for emotional relationships. When they do, they can set such impossible standards for others to meet that they push even the people they love most away. When they start looking for replacements they run into difficulties because their 'halos' are often off-putting to ordinary mortals!

Burn-out

Perfectionists are so focused on achieving the very best outcome in everything they do that their bodies often crack under the strain. Even when they have a 'day off', in an effort to get the very best bargain or the perfect fit they will 'shop till they drop'.

Being Stuck in a Rut

Obsessive behaviour strangles spontaneity and creativity. Perfectionists are so busy with their demanding life in the present that they haven't time to sit back and ponder new ideas. Their brains (worn out by a continual diet of worry and guilt) have a tendency to go blank if requested to do anything out of the ordinary.

Change induces panic in them, partly because of their exhaustion and partly because they cannot cope with the risk of mistakes and failure. Even if it means that they miss out on exciting new advances they will opt to stay with what they know.

There are many different reasons why people become too perfectionist. A common one is that their self-esteem reserves are too low. They chase perfect outcomes as a way of bolstering their self-worth. Very often they are trying to please others in the hope that they will receive praise, love or attention. Sometimes they have spent too much time around other perfectionists and developed the belief that nothing is worth doing unless it is done 'properly'. Alternatively, they could still be smarting internally from a past hurt or mistake, or indeed from current emotional pain. Obsessive behaviour is often used as a way of channelling troublesome feelings.

If any of these reasons are ringing bells for you, you will need to set aside some time to work on whatever is feeding your perfectionist driver. This may involve just some simple self-esteem boosting, or it could mean finding yourself a counsellor or self-help group to help you look at buried emotional pain. In the meantime, you could start to try and get your perfectionism under control by establishing some 'good enough indicators' for the majority of your everyday tasks.

Please note that we understand that it is too much to ask perfectionists to give up their quest for excellence in every area of their lives. (Indeed, that would increase rather than decrease their internal pressure!) But we do suggest that you should strive to find some way of measuring when you have reached an acceptable point of perfection. We know this is often extremely hard to do; you may need to monitor yourself for a few months and gain the opinion of relevant other people.

Establishing 'good enough indicators' is however a little easier, so that is why we suggest you do this task first. We will first talk about the ones we use for ourselves, to illustrate how these can help.

When reviewing his life after realizing that he was becoming stressed, Malcolm identified that he was increasing his pressure by trying to be a perfect parent. One of the symptoms was that he was striving always to ensure that no child was ever alone. Having four children, he was obviously setting himself a near-impossible task. He decided that he ought to drop his standards to 'good enough'. His first 'good enough indicator' was to spend an hour a night with each child, and two hours each day at the weekends. This of course filled up virtually his whole existence. Therefore he had to set a more realistic 'good enough indicator', which was that on any one evening he had to make sure that at least half an hour was spent with three of his four children.

Within his chosen profession as a research scientist, for many years Malcolm was driven to publish papers at the rate of one a week. This put enormous pressure on him, as he was continuously having to churn out original research, often hurriedly, and sometimes consequently of limited quality. His 'good enough indicator' initially became two papers a month, then one a month, and now it is six a year.

Within the area of personal enjoyment, Malcolm used to fill every weekend up with activities so that something had to be done on a Friday night, Saturday morning, afternoon and evening, and Sunday morning, afternoon and evening, which meant at least seven activities every weekend! He has now reduced this to a total of three activities – one for himself, one for his children, and one for his relationship.

Gael has now decided that she will allow herself to 'go for gold' when she is writing books. This means that she can spend as long as her publishers can stand perfecting her manuscripts. She will allow herself to re-write and re-write even through holiday times and weekends when she has a deadline to meet. However, in order to earn a reasonable living she has to ensure that in much of her other work she is only aiming for 'silver' standard or 'good enough'. So she now sets 'good enough indicators' for many of her projects before starting. These are usually a set number of hours or days for preparing or doing the piece of work.

But where Gael has saved most time and energy is in accepting 'good enough indicators' within her home. This was very important as she works most of the time at home. Now she firmly tells herself that if the kitchen surfaces and bathrooms are clean, she can start a day in her office without doing two hours of housework first!

Another area where Gael was able to reduce her pressure was in her personal care. For years she had been forcing herself to do innumerable kinds of physical exercise in the form of sports and attending gyms. These she found very time-consuming and not very enjoyable. She would often skip her classes and then put more pressure on herself by feeling guilty! So she decided that if she did 20 minutes of physical exercise five mornings a week at home, and stayed below a certain (secret!) dress size, that would indicate that her exercise routine was *good enough*.

Now it's your turn! We suggest that if you are experiencing a good deal of difficulty in managing your time and pressures at the moment, you should do the following exercise on a certain day each month for six months. At the end of this time you should be feeling the benefits and will have started automatically reassessing your needs and priorities whenever there is a change in your life or you begin to feel too pressurized.

ⒺXERCISE

My 'good enough indicators' and priorities.

Using the headings below, list common tasks which you have to perform when you are functioning in each area of your life. (Restrict yourself to no more than 10 under each heading!) Include some important ones, but also many smaller minor ones.

1 Work
2 Personal care
3 Family

4 Social life
5 Other

Now choose the three tasks which you consider need to be done to an excellent (Gold Star) standard.

Then choose another three for which you and others could (or should!) accept an above-average standard (Silver Star).

Beside each of the rest, make a note of a 'good enough indicator' (a sign that you have reached an acceptable standard).

Using the headings, make a prioritized 'to do' list for the next month, and beside each item allocate the number of minutes, hours or days you intend to spend on each one.

Add up the total number of hours you have programmed for these tasks and assess whether or not you have given yourself too much or too little pressure.

Having read this chapter and (we hope!) completed the exercises, you may have concluded that you do not need or want to change your life at all. When this happens to us (as it indeed often does now), we still do not consider the time we have spent on our Review as being wasted. We find that the reflection has helped us to become more accepting of our pressures because we have made a clear and considered choice to keep them in our lives. And of course, once you have accepted responsibility for your load it is much easier to motivate yourself to manage it more sensibly!

MY PERFECTIONISM IS UNDER MY CONTROL.

I RESPECT MY NEEDS AND PRIORITIES.

3

REFUSE

Decreasing the demands on yourself involves a number of different strategies and thought processes, but perhaps the most important of all is to become an expert at refusing!

In order to remain *Positive Under Pressure* we must ensure that we can (and do!) refuse to:

- do what we don't need to do
- do what we don't want to do
- do what we know we will do badly
- do what other people can do better
- do anything just because someone has asked us to do it
- continue to do something just because we have started to do it
- say more than we want to
- explain or justify when we don't need to
- argue when we haven't the time or energy to do so.

In addition to the many demands on your life from work and family, you probably have a great number in your social activities as well. If you are a sports person it is likely that you will be committed not just to playing the odd game, but to fit in a fuller schedule than most other people. If you like going to evening classes, you are likely to have signed up for far more than you'll ever realistically make. All this is probably in addition to the community work you have promised to do. We are amazed at how many people on our courses are on local committees for the church, the youth club, the school, the RSPCA, the hikers' club, the action committee to stop the road being widened, etc., etc. And of course not only are you likely to be involved in activities such as these, you are probably on the committee, and well on the road to becoming chair, secretary or events organizer as well!

Even if this doesn't sound like your life, you may be feeling guilty that it isn't, or wishing that it was!

In the last chapter we looked at the importance of reviewing your pressure load and reassessing your needs and priorities. This is vital preparatory work for refusing. We have to be clear which tasks and roles we aim to do perfectly and which ones we can accept a 'good enough' standard for. In short, in order to say 'No' quickly and effectively, we must:

1 Know our Nows – so we can say Yes
2 Know our Nexts – so we can say Not Yet
3 Know our Nevers – so we can say NO-NO-NO!

If you did the exercise on page 109, first take a look at what you wrote or thought about then. If you didn't, do the exercise now before doing this next one.

⊖XERCISE

In order to reduce your pressure, list three things (under each of the headings below) which you would like to refuse to do or say. As a guide and memory jogger we have included some examples shared by participants on our courses – but remember the kind of thing or person you may need to refuse may be very different.

Tick the ones which you would find difficult to refuse.

Mark each with a number: 1, 2 or 3 – that is, is it a NOW (1), NEXT (2) or NEVER (3)?

Core Role at Work

working late every night

attending unnecessary meetings

taking full minutes when brief notes would do

seeing more clients, patients or customers than you can give
    good attention to

writing unnecessary reports

having breakfast meetings

Associated Work Roles

being on the social committee

attending certain conferences

giving media interviews

writing other people's letters

listening to a surfeit of other people's problems

sharing a minute-by-minute account of your weekend activities

going to an office 'do'

repairing cheap office property

Family Life

cooking every night when you can afford to eat out or have
    take-aways

engaging in the same old circular arguments

acting as family chauffeur on demand

doing Dad's garden when he just moans and never says
    'Thank-you'

spending a stressful Christmas with members of your family
    out of misplaced duty rather than love or compassion

writing cards and letters to relatives who don't need or want
    to hear from you

mowing the lawn/cleaning the house more often than it needs

going on shopping expeditions when it's only your plastic
    cards that are welcome

Friendships

engaging in gossip or chat that bores or irritates you
spending time with friends with whom you now have little in
    common
going to places you do not want to go to
drinking more or for longer than you want because your
    friends do

Leisure Activities

engaging in more practice for your sport than you can afford
    to do
waiting around to give people lifts home from the theatre
    when they can easily afford taxis
'after-event' socializing with your personal trainer/squash
    partner/darts team
seeing films that are of little interest to you
going out when you would rather have a night at home

Community Activities

distributing leaflets when you'd rather pay someone to do so
sitting on time-wasting committees
writing a complaint each time you receive poor service
raising money for every charity you support

I ALWAYS KNOW MY NOWS,

NEXTS AND NEVERS.

Why You May Not Be Saying 'No' When You Want To

Although you will be aware that it is easier for you to say 'Yes'
than to say 'No,' you may not understand the root of your

problem. We have found that it is helpful to give this a little thought. When we ask people on our courses to give this some thought, these are some of the responses:

I don't want people to think I'm selfish.

It's mean not to help other people.

I would want people always to say 'Yes' when I ask them to do something.

It helps them feel better.

I hate to upset people.

I feel guilty if I am not helping.

Those who have perhaps slightly more insight have said things such as:

When I am helping other people, I don't have time to think about my own problems.

It's better to be too busy and stressed, than to have time I don't know what to do with.

And one, who was a Senior Registrar in Psychiatry and had just completed a course which required him to do some serious professional navel-gazing, said 'It validates my own existence and is a natural consequence of my Jungian extroversion.' (We're not even sure we know what he meant!)

It is up to you how far you want to take your self-analysis, but we hope that you will do enough to realize that you were *not* born 'just a girl (or boy!) who can't say No'.

SAYING 'NO' IS PARTLY AN ART AND PARTLY
A HABIT. WITH PRACTICE I CAN LEARN HOW
TO DO IT WELL AND MORE OFTEN.

Later in this chapter we will introduce you to an assertiveness technique to help you perfect the art of saying 'No', but for the moment let's look at the habit aspect.

You may be agreeing to do and say many things simply because you have always done so. (Or it seems as though you have always done so.) Saying 'Yes' automatically in response to a request may be a habit you picked up at a very early age. Perhaps you had very 'nice' parents who always martyred themselves for others and you simply learned that style of behaviour from them. Or, perhaps by chance, as a child you found that saying 'Yes' increased the flow of love or attention when it was in short supply. Perhaps you were too frightened or too in awe to say 'No'. Or maybe (like Gael, as a convent school girl) you had the impression that you needed to say 'Yes' to everyone to secure your place in heaven. Malcolm now realizes that the root of his saying 'Yes' is that he believed people would like him. He believes he learned at school that if you said 'No' to people they shunned you, whereas if you said 'Yes' to people they welcomed you into the fold.

Many people take programmed habits into adulthood without even realizing it. Others may be aware that they have certainly taken this behaviour well past its 'sell-by-date' but they still find themselves automatically saying 'Yes' in the heat of the moment. Once they have done this they then feel committed to following through on their 'promise' even though they may know that agreeing was an unwise and inappropriate reflex response.

On the other hand, your automatic response may be one which has developed in your adult life. You may have spent too long, for example, working or studying in highly regulated, authoritarian organizations which do not take or tolerate 'No' for an answer.

Alternatively, you may have spent many years being paid to be a 'Yes' person because being so was considered 'good practice' and appropriate to your role. Many people we have worked with in the service industries or caring and customer-based professions have developed their unassertive habits in this way. Fortunately, these professions are changing and some are even employing trainers like us to teach their staff to say 'No'! This change is usually welcomed by the vast majority of staff including directors, even if it originally has been 'forced' upon management. More and more people even in the most hard-edged industries are becoming aware that a career in martyrdom is not very attractive to the best potential recruits. They have also discovered, through research, that they were paying an extortionately high price for prematurely burning out their most dedicated staff.

Two experiences from corporate courses we have run illustrate this point well.

The first corporate course was run for Hospital Trust administrators, both clinical and non-clinical, and the consultants working for them. When people were asked to commit to when they were next going to practise their assertiveness skills, and say 'No' when they would have usually said 'Yes,' one of the consultants present said that the next time he was asked to attend an early morning meeting, he would say 'No.' Another said the next time he was asked to be on a committee which decided on an aspect of hospital management that he did not think was important (he gave the example of furnishings in the out-patients room), he would say 'No.'

Both these consultants agreed that their Clinical Director's philosophy was to overwork people and to expect them to do more than they felt able. The Clinical Director, who was sitting right there, burst out laughing at this point, and produced from his briefcase a memo that he had just written informing all the other directors and hospital management that, in his opinion, these two consultants were trying to get themselves on to every committee, and he felt their clinical tasks were suffering as a result.

It is amazing how people, even when academically intelligent, can miss completely the amount of internal pressure they mistake for external pressure.

The other insight that came from one of our corporate courses originated with a Human Resources Director. This woman had told Malcolm, when they were selecting which modules from the *Positive Under Pressure* workshops would be incorporated into the day's programme, that they did not want any assertiveness modules because after a previous assertiveness course all the staff had resolved to refuse to do certain tasks. However, as the workshop progressed the staff felt free and safe enough in the facilitated group environment to talk about not having enough time, and how they wished they could decrease some of their activities at home and at work. When asked to suggest when they would next assertively refuse, it was evident that they were all steering clear of cutting down their work activities, as they all gave examples from their home life.

One of the loudest cheers we ever heard on our courses was when the Human Resources Director herself stood up and said she wanted to give not just one example, but three. The first was she was going to refuse her own drive to stay late at work three nights a week. The second was she was going to refuse any meetings, for her and her staff, which were scheduled before the working day officially began. And the third was that when any of her staff asked her to read a report in an unrealistic time frame she would say 'No.' The cheers turned to laughter when she said that she had also learned one thing she was never going to refuse again, which was the offer of help for her own assertiveness!

But old habits die hard, especially those that have been around a long time and have previously been well rewarded. So we suggest that you don't wait for them to die a natural death. (You could be waiting a lifetime!) Instead, you have to beat them with proactive strategies which will work at both a conscious and unconscious level.

Accept that there is little point in trying to stop the requests in the first place. As a high achiever or potentially high achiever, you will continue to be asked to do things more often than most people. The plus side of this (which we must never take for granted) is that you attract many more opportunities. The potentially negative aspect is that you can give yourself too much pressure if you are not very selective.

You must be ready and willing to say 'No' firmly and frequently.

Three Ways to Say 'No'

1/Firm Up Your Right to Say 'No'

We have found that affirming your appropriate right to refuse over and over again has been a very useful way for many people to overcome the 'Yes' habit. The rights that you may need to affirm could be legal or simply basic human prerogatives.

The technique is simple: Simply repeat out loud in an assertive, authoritative tone a statement such as one of the ones we have listed in the exercise below. When you next find you are in a situation where your right to say 'No' is under threat, you will find that your affirmation statement immediately pops up from your subconscious into your conscious mind as a reminder. As a result, you feel more empowered to refuse.

Many people tell us that when these affirmations are at work it is like having an imaginary friend sitting on their shoulder whispering into their ear. We trust that in the long term you will not need any tricks of the imagination to help you Refuse to do anything which will cause you unnecessary stress.

❸XERCISE

This exercise incorporates some examples which other people have used and found effective.

As you read this list of rights, mark the ones which have some meaning for you.

- I have the right not to get involved in someone else's problems.
- I have the right to be treated with respect.
- I have the right to justice.
- I have the right to protect my health.
- I have the right to protect my privacy.
- I have the right to a balanced lifestyle.
- I have the right to have fun.
- I have the right to choose my friends.
- I have the right to choose with whom I spend my leisure time.
- I have the right to dislike certain films or books.
- I have the right to choose a certain level of fitness.
- I have the right to be just 'good enough' sometimes.

Add any others which are relevant for you.

Beside each right, note what price you could pay if you continue to abuse this right for yourself by not saying 'NO' when you need to do so.

For example:

> I have the right to a balanced lifestyle – if I don't learn to say 'No' sometimes I could lose my family or destroy my health.

Choose three rights to concentrate on for the next few weeks. Write these out on a card and pin them up somewhere.

2/Practise Refusing Unimportant Requests

Flex your Refusal muscles gently at first. For the first week or so of your 'campaign', try some simple refusals in your everyday life, even when it would do you little harm to say 'Yes.' For example, say 'No' to having the window open or an extra helping of food or a lift from a friend or taking a leaflet in a store. Remember to use a very **calm, self-assured tone and make direct (but not staring) eye contact** with the other person.

This kind of practice will help you to get used to saying the word 'No' or 'No, thank you' very naturally and comfortably. Try not to give any unnecessary justifications or apologies. If you must say 'sorry', say it only once. If you feel uncomfortable or guilty afterwards, simply repeat an appropriate right several times. (*I have the right to choose what I want to buy and when I want to buy it.*)

I ONLY SAY SORRY ONCE.

If you still feel uncomfortable, share your feelings with a supportive friend as soon as you can. They may probably help you to have a laugh at yourself, which should help you to gain some perspective.

Be careful to choose situations where there is no 'hidden agenda' which might suddenly surface. It is probably safer to practise saying 'No' to strangers rather than to people with whom you work or live. If not, you could find yourself in unexpected deep water, as indeed Malcolm did when he first tried this exercise:

Many years ago, as a recovering caffeine addict, Malcolm decided that he would say 'No' when his secretary asked him if he wanted a cup of coffee in the morning. The conversation went something like this:

SECRETARY: 'Malcolm, would you like a cup of coffee?'
MALCOLM: 'No thank you, I don't want one.'
SECRETARY: 'I said, do you want a cup of coffee?'
MALCOLM: 'No thank you, I don't want one.'

His secretary's voice was slowly raised to almost a shout: 'Malcolm, I said do you want a cup of coffee?'

MALCOLM (*staying calm*): 'No, I don't want one.'
SECRETARY (*exploding*): 'What's wrong with my coffee?'

MALCOLM (*still calm*): 'There's nothing wrong with your coffee, I just don't want one.'

SECRETARY: 'You've never liked my coffee, have you? And what's more, you haven't liked the way I have worked for you for the past year, have you?'

Fortunately there was in the end a happy ending to this ironic and rather humorous tale. This difficult conversation led to Malcolm being able to acknowledge openly that he had not liked some of his secretary's behaviour. They then proceeded to talk sensibly and professionally about their relationship and mutual expectations and needs. As a result, they negotiated a much better way of working together. But this was not the outcome Malcolm had expected, and certainly was *not* the best way to start off practising saying 'No'!

We advise you, therefore, to keep your initial practice for door-to-door salespeople or requests in the street from market researchers who are well trained in handling refusals.

3/Repeat Your Refusal Persistently

We teach a very simple standard assertiveness training technique which is generally called 'Broken Record'. It was given this name because it was first identified as a technique in the days when vinyl records were what we all listened to. As you'll know, a scratched record plays the same phrase over and over again.

The essence of the technique is that, instead of making excuses, telling lies, saying 'No/sorry/sorry/sorry/sorry' or just giving in and saying 'Yes,' you do the following.

1 Select **a simple phrase or sentence** such as 'No thank you, I don't want to do that' to be your key Broken Record statement.

2 In response to any arguments, requests, questions or demands for justification, simply **repeat this statement in a**

steady, calm tone over and over again until the person you are refusing gets the message that you mean it.

Any parent knows only too well that children play Broken Record absolutely naturally. Perhaps even if you don't have children you have heard the power of their repeated phrases in a park or queue. For example:

Mum, can I have an ice cream? Can I have an ice cream? Can I have an ice cream? . . . etc., etc.

You can probably remember the sound of the constant repetitions even now, because they have a tendency to stick in our heads. At the time they often feel a little mesmerizing. Your hearing becomes selective and you notice only the repeated phrase. You cannot ignore it. Inevitably, at some point, if only to regain your 'peace of mind' you feel the compulsion to 'turn it off'. Over-pressurized parents commonly 'turn off' their children's Broken Record by either giving in or becoming aggressively authoritarian. A few enlightened ones will of course realize what is happening and 'Broken Record their children back' in a stronger, firmer (but still calm and controlled) voice.

Unfortunately, by the time most of us reach adulthood our Broken Record skills have been 'socialized' out of us. So most people have to re-learn them (especially if they have children or work or live with childlike adults!). When they do, they often become very excited at having reclaimed this powerful tool. We can both remember the first time we picked up this technique again through assertiveness training. For a while, we both became Broken Record junkies. We used the technique too often and too crudely and, as a result, we gave ourselves more, not less pressure. In response to our blunt refusals we would get an adult equivalent of a 'clip around the ear' or alternatively, we would hear a martyred voice responding 'Oh all right, if you must' which, of course, we knew meant we were heading for big trouble later!

We therefore had to learn to adapt and modify the technique to suit our more sophisticated adult world. We found that using it in conjunction with two other kinds of statements – the **empathy statement** and a **negotiation or compromise** – made it much more effective and led to much less trouble.

An **empathy statement** can preface your refusal. It's a sentence which indicates that you have taken the other person's feelings or situation into account. In the examples that follow we have put the key Broken Record statement in **bold face type**, while the empathy statement is in *italics*.

> *It must be hard for you to have nothing to do tomorrow, so I understand why you are asking me to go to the cinema with you*, but **I don't want to go**.

> *I appreciate that you are feeling overburdened* as well, but **I cannot accept any more work today**.

> *I understand that you think we should meet once more* before submitting the report, but **I cannot fit in another meeting this week**.

And in these next examples, the negotiation or compromise elements are in *italics* (the Broken Record statement remains in **bold**).

> **I don't want to go to the cinema tomorrow**, but *I'd be happy to get our diaries together next week and see if we can meet for lunch*.

> As I have already said, **I cannot accept any more work today**, but *I would be pleased to meet with you next week* to talk through both roles.

> **I cannot fit in another meeting this week**. *It's OK by me if you do a further edit and then fax it to me. I will then look at it first thing on Monday*.

In relation to managing pressure, we have found that in most situations an offer to negotiate or compromise is not necessary. Most people who need to learn this technique are already doing more than their fair share, or have been generally much too 'nice' or are attempting to be too perfect. When others around you see that you have started to Refuse, they may be surprised, but they rarely object for long. (Perhaps partly because you have activated their guilt buttons!)

So, remember, more often than not a polite assertive Refusal is all that is needed. If that doesn't work you can try adding an empathy statement several times to your Broken Record statement, before offering to negotiate or compromise.

We also recommend that you start practising the Broken Record technique in situations where it is not too risky for you to Refuse. Your anxiety levels will be much more manageable and you will be more likely to be able to persist. Once you have become convinced of the power of the technique, you will want to use it in more tricky situations.

But of course, in practice we know that, however simple and effective this technique is, you are likely to come across problems in using it. So here is a trouble-shooting guide for the most common questions we are asked.

What Happens If Two People 'Broken Record' Each Other?

Usually at some point you both break out in a smile. Assertive people like meeting other assertive people. They have immediate respect for each other even though they may not always agree. Their mutual smiles are usually followed by an offer of compromise. If not, the two agree to differ and seek help towards negotiating from a third party. Alternatively, they may agree to 'fight it out' at some later date when each has had more time to find adequate 'ammunition' for their case or additional 'troops' (supportive friends or colleagues). If one person ends up winning, at least the other usually feels better than they would have done if they had 'given in' at the very beginning. Their self-esteem has not been damaged because they have 'done their best', been treated with respect, and had their case heard. In a work situation, their assertive behaviour has probably been noticed and admired and will almost certainly be rewarded sometime later.

What Happens When the Person Is a Friend and Becomes Upset?

If a friend persists in attempts to make you change your mind, then he or she is guilty of abusing your rights. If this person persists in doing so in spite of your Broken Record, regard that behaviour as an indication that the terms of the friendship may need to be looked at and 'renegotiated' sometime soon. (But not now!) Privately resolve to address this later and continue to use the Broken Record technique, perhaps with more empathy than you would do normally.

If your friend then begins to resort to emotional blackmail by saying 'I really need you to come' or starts threatening you by saying 'If you don't come with me this time, I won't do something you want next time', remind yourself that it is never helpful to give in to manipulative or aggressive behaviour. (You are simply setting yourself up for further abuse later on.) Should your friend then 'up the stakes' by threatening never to see you again, you have to question whether you really want this type of person as a friend. But, once again, don't be tempted to get hooked into saying any of this right at the moment. Just continue to Broken Record with less empathy and do not offer compromise!

Later, in 'the cold light of day', review the friendship. Good friendship is, after all, about giving people the space and support they need without being demanding, manipulative or threatening.

I DO NOT WASTE ENERGY BEING DRAWN
INTO AN ARGUMENT AGAINST MY WILL.

What Happens If Your Guilt Button Gets Pressed?

This is a very common ploy among manipulators and aggressors when they are stone-walled by Broken Record. We call this the

'Apples are Apples and Pears are Pears' syndrome. For example, when you say 'No thank you, I don't want to go to the cinema tonight' (Apples), they reply by saying, 'But I went shopping with you last week' (Pears). They have introduced a factor which is not relevant in this instance. Don't fall for it! Don't get drawn into the argument. Don't be tempted even to say, 'It is not relevant that you came with me last week.'

You could, however, convert their 'Pear' into your empathetic statement 'I know it must be difficult for you as you came with me last week, but on this occasion I don't want to go.' What is important is that we don't confuse the 'Apples' (you not wanting to come this time) with the 'Pears' (they came with you last time).

Be careful, too, about giving excuses. They are usually not necessary and perhaps not justified if the other person is abusing your rights. Once you give an excuse you are giving the person the lever to begin to alter your wishes. For example 'I have to go home on time tonight because I must take the children swimming.' They can (and often do!) find the answer for you that suits them. They might say 'You could get them a taxi just this once. I know them – they wouldn't mind. They know you love them and they'd understand because you are doing a favour for a friend.'

Never forget that this sort of ploy could put you in an even more pressurized situation, backed into a corner with nowhere to go – especially if they have already started dialling the taxi company or even your children!

If instead you just say 'I don't want to' in a strong calm voice, they receive a clear message that you are being guided by your feelings and that logical argument is not appropriate. Giving them an excuse, in effect, gives them a mixed message because it indicates that there is a case to be argued and, what is more, it gives them some free ammunition with which to continue the discussion.

What Happens If You Start to Feel Sorry for the Other Person?

This is a tricky one that always surfaces on every course we run. We would like to make it very clear that we are not in favour of anyone abusing the rights of anyone else. We also trust that you are not interested in doing that either. The rights which we wish to have for ourselves must also be rights we would expect others to have as well. If, however, in certain circumstances we find that our rights do come in direct conflict with other people's needs, refusing may not be the best option. You must be prepared to negotiate or occasionally back down. If you are continually making this choice, however, you have to be prepared to take responsibility for the possible consequences (that is, burnout). Burnout rarely hurts only the person concerned, it has a negative ripple effect on many others, especially when the stressed-out person has some kind of caring or management role.

If you find yourself persistently unable to refuse simply because you don't want to hurt others, you need to do some serious life-reviewing or self-esteem building.

What If a Third Party Is Going to Be Hurt by My Refusal?

This is a favourite question posed to us by doctors and many other professionals who consider their jobs to be 'special cases' where Refusal is not an option. This is the kind of example they give us:

> Two very tired over-worked doctors are just about to go home (late, of course) when there is a knock on the surgery door. Outside there is a patient who is bleeding profusely. Refusing to help may mean that the patient could die or become much more seriously ill. Both think that this patient should be seen by the other person. They both have pressing engagements at home.
>
> This, we are told, is an everyday story of a contemporary doctor's life. They argue that Refusal is never an option for them because work gives them special responsibilities in relation to the care of others.
>
> Our response is that they should not get into an argument, but just try practising the technique in case they ever have a

need to use it. Alternatively, we suggest that it could be a useful tool to teach their patients.

Fortunately, after they have had a good dose of relaxation, support and mild confrontation by the end of the course, they are thinking much more optimistically and logically. They are able to accept that, although bleeding patients at the door cannot be refused, they are in fact very rare and not a good reason for saying 'Yes' to many other refusable tasks. They agree that in the extreme situation they quoted one person may have to capitulate, but careful record-keeping and good staff reviews and assertive communication can ensure that the burden is shared fairly.

So, if you find yourself using the 'special case' argument too often, you definitely need this dose of *Positive Under Pressure*! In the short term the answer is, of course, don't use Broken Record to deal with any kind of emergency. Deal with it, note it and put the questions it raises on an agenda for later discussion. You can use Broken Record or Scripting (see page 136) later to help you make sure that the problem gets the hearing it deserves.

WHEN I REFUSE I CAN STILL SHOW RESPECT
AND CONCERN FOR THE FEELINGS AND
NEEDS OF THE OTHER PERSON.

❸XERCISE

Make a list of situations in your everyday life where you could practise using Broken Record.

Mark these on a scale of 1–10 in order of the amount of risk your refusal would carry (10 if you would be likely to lose your job, 1 if your refusal would cause a raised eyebrow or two).

For each situation try to imagine how the conversation might develop. Note what kind of argument or emotional blackmail or threat the other person might use. Practise responding with an appropriate Broken Record and empathy statement. Note whether you would be willing to compromise in any of these situations.

Finally, remember that once you decide to say 'No,' your worst fears do not happen. You don't lose friendships, nor people's respect, nor your job, by saying 'No' once. If the relationship is essentially good, refusing can in fact enhance it. If you are in the right job, saying 'No' to additional work can similarly have a beneficial effect. The person asking understands that you know your capabilities and your limitations, and your realistic workload, and they will respect you more for this. Perhaps your saying 'No' is likely to give somebody else the opportunity to do the job which they may do better than you, or they may need to do as a learning experience. Your saying 'No' may be the best thing that you have done for yourself and others.

> TO DO THE BEST I CAN FOR YOU, I HAVE
> TO DO THE VERY BEST I CAN FOR ME.

You will undoubtedly be a better partner, workmate, friend, relative or parent if you start to reduce the demands on yourself.

> I DO NOT USE MY ASSERTIVE POWER
> TO ABUSE OTHERS.

4

RESOURCE

As we have said earlier, pressure is simply a mis-match between our demands and resources. When we perceive that we do not have the means to cope with what we need to do, we begin to feel uncomfortable and respond adversely. As Charles Dickens' Mr Micawber says in the novel *David Copperfield*: 'Annual income twenty pounds, annual expenditure nineteen ninety six, result happiness. Annual income twenty pounds, annual expenditure twenty pounds ought and six, result misery.' So don't forget that for you to feel better and start acting in a positive rather than a negative way, your resources only have to be slightly above your demands!

Your demands may be self-imposed, or imposed by other people. They may be very real, such as having bills to pay, jobs to complete or children to feed and clothe. But they could be unrealistic expectations 'cooked up' in our own or other people's minds. (Remember our work on perfectionism in the Review chapter, for example.)

Very commonly, the resource we lack most today is time, but for some of you it could be money, support or emotional strength. These too can be genuine shortages – such as being given a totally unrealistic schedule by a demanding boss, being unable to pay your bills, or suffering the loss of a close and trusted friend – or they can be imagined, as when we are tired or off-colour and perceive our resources in a more negative way than we do when we are feeling great.

Other important factors affecting our perception of our own demands and resources are, of course, our personality, personal history and individual circumstances. Some people think having to do five tasks in a day is a lot. Others would think the same number of tasks to be just a few. Some would rather do only two, whereas others would be happy doing 20. When it comes to writing letters, some people may think writing 10 at one sitting is impossible, while others are happy to write twice as many. If our children want to be driven to school every day, some people are pleased to do this while others find it a drain on their time. If our parents want to visit once a week, some people are pleased, others disappointed that it is not three times a week, while others wish it was more like once a year!

Similarly with regard to resources, if some of us have a thousand pounds, dollars or yen in the bank, we think ourselves rich. Others might panic at having 'only' this much, and imagine themselves heading for skid row. Equally, some of us are more able to function with minimum support, whereas others need to feel part of a team or need to have constant reassurance.

So before looking at how you can increase your resources you may need to check that your pressure is not being caused by a distorted perception of the demands you face. You can start by talking to someone who is in a position to view both your demands and resources in an objective manner. But please remember to try to avoid:

people who are close to you. Your family and your friends are
    likely to be affected by their emotional involvement with
    you
colleagues who may have competing or similar pressures
anyone who is in a state of stress

anyone who may be too scared or unassertive to give you direct, honest feedback.

If your 'advisor' disagrees with your perception, but fails to convince you, stop and take some time out before rushing headlong into a potentially stressful battle to obtain more of what you think you need. Re-read and work once again on some of the exercises and strategies given in the chapters on the first three Rs (Relax, Review, Refuse).

Doing this preparatory work will increase your chances of succeeding in your next task, which is to start designing an action plan to increase your resources. We suggest that this should cover the following three areas:

1 reviewing the way your resources are currently being managed to see if they can be used more efficiently
2 developing your ethical powers of persuasion to ask more forcibly for what you need
3 stimulating your creativity and expanding your horizons to increase your sources of help.

Let's look at each of these areas in turn.

Review Your Resources/Check Your Efficiency

It is likely that if the balance between your demands and resources is out of kilter, you have been what we call 'fire-fighting' with life for some time. You have probably been dealing only with the urgent tasks and leaving the more mundane ones for a calmer time. Of course this is a great temporary policy, but one which many people who like living in the fast lane of life tend to carry on for far too long. We tend to hate doing the less exciting background work (such as filing, sorting, balancing the books and cleaning), which in the long run helps to make us function in any area of life much more efficiently. Our pressure increases as we often have to find even more resources to:

- replace things we have lost
- apologize for forgotten appointments and birthdays
- repair badly maintained appliances and vehicles
- pay interest on overdue accounts
- re-write the non-backed-up reports our crashed computer 'lost'
- deal with the 'tantrums' of neglected children
- recover from the sicknesses our worn-out bodies couldn't resist.

Have we started to ring your internal bells?! If so, deal with your guilt instantly by taking a moment to do this exercise.

ⒺXERCISE

Answer these following two questions:

1 Over the last month, have I depleted my resources in any of these areas by, for example, using more of either my own or others' time, money or energy than I should have needed to use if I were being super-efficient? (If so, note down some examples. Write down enough to convince and motivate you, but not enough to throw you into a deep depression!)
   my personal care
   my working life
   my family commitments
   my community life
   my hobbies and sports
   my financial commitments
   the care of my home
   the care of my appliances/vehicles
2 Which six actions will I take during the next month to

ensure that I use the resources which I already have more efficiently?

> I REGULARLY CHECK THAT MY RESOURCES
> ARE BEING USED EFFICIENTLY.

Develop Your Powers of Persuasion

When we are under pressure we often tend to take the quickest route to acquiring new resources. This means that even the most assertive among us find ourselves behaving in either a manipulative or an aggressive way in order to persuade others to give us what we want. In the short term, methods such as pleading, emotional blackmail or threatening demands may work much more quickly. But do they leave you feeling very good about yourself? And do they leave the people who give you what you want feeling like helping you again? After the crisis is over, you may well end up spending a good deal of extra time and energy dealing with your guilt and repairing your relationships. So resist the temptation and brush up your persuasive skills.

There are two techniques which we find invaluable. The first is Broken Record, which we already used in our chapter on Refuse (page 111).

Broken Record

Here is an example of this technique being used in an office situation. Note that Angela's Broken Record statement is in **bold face**, while her empathy statement is in *italics*.

ANGELA: The amount of sickness in the office means that **I must have an extra temp on Friday**.

BILL: That's impossible. I can't put in a request. I'm up to my eyes in work this week.

ANGELA: *I appreciate that it is difficult for you*, but **I must have a temp on Friday**.

BILL: Can't you hang on until next Wednesday? I could do
the application over the weekend.

ANGELA: No. **I must have the temp by Friday.**

BILL: Don't you think this job is difficult enough without
being put under this kind of pressure?

ANGELA: *I know there are many difficulties with your job and
I hope the pressure eases off soon,* but the fact remains that **I
must have a temp on Friday**.

BILL: Oh, OK, if you insist, but the whole staffing policy will
be discussed at the next board meeting, and I'll want a full
report from you.

ANGELA: Agreed – thanks a lot.

Scripting

The second of our techniques is called Scripting. This is a tightly
structured way of preparing the first minute or two of a verbal
request. As you know, the first minute or two of any communication is the most vital. During this time we set the tone for the
conversation; it is very difficult to shift out of this tone once it
is set. In these first few moments we must therefore make sure
that we:

- establish the impression that we are somebody whose needs
  and wishes must be taken seriously
- establish a positive, upbeat tone, because we know that
  people are much more likely to respond favourably if we do
- indicate that we have respect for the other person and have
  empathy with their feelings and needs.

We have found that, when you first start Scripting the opening
of your request, it is best to do it in writing. This gives you a
chance to edit and re-edit until you have as concise and punchy
a request as you can. If it is an important request and you know
you are emotionally charged up about it, it is also advisable to

get someone to help you to compose your Script and listen and watch you rehearsing it.

An added advantage of making a habit of writing Scripts out beforehand is that you will automatically find that you begin to use this method for making written request in letters and reports as well.

Guidelines for Scripting the Opening of Your Request

These are the four key steps which must be written or said, in the order which we suggest. We have given two examples, one from an office situation and the other from a personal experience at home.

Step 1 is to **give a concise summarized explanation** of your problem. Use objective language (don't include feelings or impressions) and keep to the point (restrict yourself to one point at a time, whenever possible). Don't give reasons why you think the problems have occurred. (You could do this later, if appropriate and necessary):

> The demand for this product has far exceeded the figures I estimated in the planning meeting last June.

> The dishwasher has been broken for three weeks now, and I have been doing the dishes six out of seven nights this week, but tonight I must do the ironing.

Finally, be sure to omit unnecessary justifications or apologies. One sincere 'sorry' is usually quite adequate. Over-apologizing doesn't tend to endear you to resource-givers, as they are often busy assertive people themselves.

Step 2 is to **acknowledge the feelings** which the shortage of resources and your request has, or may, arouse in both yourself and the person to whom you are making the request. Be careful to use words which are appropriate to the situation. Make an appropriate statement acknowledging your own feelings, then empathize with the other persons' feelings or situation. Use a matter-of-fact tone to avoid sounding patronizing.

I feel guilty for having misjudged the demand, and can understand that it will be difficult for you to ask for an increase in the budget.

I feel unhappy about asking you to help. I know you are worried about your revision for tomorrow.

Step 3 is to **state your needs**. Specify the resources as precisely as you can, in one or two sentences. If more information is needed, offer it in writing or say that you will provide it later. Offer a compromise if appropriate.

I need three extra members of staff and three more computers over the next six months. I have costed my request in detail in this report.

I would like you to wash the dishes, but you can leave them to drain and then I will put them away when I have done the ironing.

Step 4 is to **spell out the positive consequences** for the other person if they meet your request. Finish your 'Script' on a positive note by outlining the 'rewards' the other person can expect from giving you what you want. These could be financial benefits, savings in time or energy, or just simply feeling good because they have helped you.

If I get these extra resources, the profit will certainly cover the cost and we won't lose these valuable new customers.

If you could just help me for half an hour before you go upstairs, I'd be so pleased and relieved.

Never threaten until you have tried this positive approach. We assure you that Scripting can work miracles, both at home and at work!

Persuasive Body Language

Don't forget that the effectiveness of any request will also be greatly affected by your non-verbal language. So make sure that you use confident, assertive body language. Here are some tips.

- Facial expression – try to ensure you look composed and in control (in spite of any internal panic!) by relaxing your brow and jaw before you speak. Be careful not to give an ingratiating smile. A genuine one is fine if it is appropriate, but your face must convey seriousness if you want your request to be heard in that spirit.
- Eyes – make direct eye contact at first, but be careful to relax it quickly. Staring makes the other person feel 'put on the spot', and they will be more likely to 'fight off' your request. Aim to maintain eye contact for about 50 per cent of the time unless you are talking to someone from a culture or background who is not used to direct eye contact.
- Stance – stand or sit upright with your shoulders down and back. Your feet should be slightly apart and both firmly placed on the ground. Your hands must be held in a comfortable, natural position and should not be fidgeting.
- Walk – your pace should be even, firm and purposeful.
- Voice – make sure that you have good projection by taking two or three deep breaths before speaking. Keep a lively pace and a warm but serious tone.

If you are submitting your request for resources in written form, don't forget that the initial impact is also very important. Your letter or report must grab the attention of the reader the moment they set eyes on it. Generally speaking, which would you rather read – a hastily scribbled note, an ungrammatical email, an over-wordy jargon-filled report or a concise, thoughtfully composed and well-spaced letter?

ⒺXERCISE

Think of a request for resources you could make in the near future, either in your personal or work life, and prepare a Script to help you ensure your request has the strongest initial impact.

> I ASK FOR WHAT I WANT IN AN
> ASSERTIVE MANNER.

Stimulate Your Creativity and Expand Your Horizons

When we are under pressure there is a great tendency to stay stuck in a rut. We tend to veer more for the safe, well-known options precisely because we are holding ourselves in an anxious, fearful state. This means that we may miss out on many sources of help which, if we were less pressured, we would have found. Sometimes people have resources right under their noses which they miss simply because they have been too set on getting help from somewhere else. Very often we find that people on our courses are not asking even their nearest and dearest for help. They may not have noticed that their children have now reached an age at which they are quite capable of doing more for themselves, or that their parents have been talking about how useless they now feel now that they are retired. Similarly, at work, some busy managers rushing around the office haven't noticed that their assistants are under-stretched or would welcome being given the chance to take on a greater challenge. (You will remember that we've noted that a common symptom of stress is a reluctance to delegate, because pressure can cause some people to develop a belief that they are indispensable.)

So, let's assume for the moment that there are many more

resources available to you than you may have noticed. What can you do to open your eyes?

First, you must relax! You cannot think creatively while whirling around on your normal merry-go-round. You have to take yourself away from the situation (either physically or mentally) and FORGET it briefly. Many of the techniques outlined in the Relax chapter will help you with this.

Secondly, do something which exercises the creative right side of your brain. This could be meditation, listening to music, drawing or exploring ideas using methods such as brainstorming or mind-maps (Tony Buzan's book, listed in the Further Reading chapter, will show you how to do this very effectively).

Thirdly, expand your horizons by looking and listening to other people. Try to find people who have *similar* (but not *the same*) pressures, and see if you can apply some of their wisdom or experience to your situation. Many big businesses who have formed strategic alliances with complementary organizations have found that they have learned a great deal from each other in this way. Also, many parents we know who have joined support groups have found that the greatest benefits to be gained are the handy hints that make everyday life so much less pressurized.

Often, it's the little extra resources or help that can make the most difference when we feel as though we are in big trouble. For example, one of the everyday pressures in Malcolm's life is when his children cannot find their school ties in the morning when they are rushing off to school. This used to be a big stress-generator for him and could set a negative tone to his whole day. Now he has overcome this by carrying a supply of spare ties in his car which can be brought out whenever a tie-crisis strikes.

Another common cause of stress for Malcolm is finding a parking space when lecturing in hospitals. So now he routinely asks someone to reserve him a space close to the lecture theatre. Gael, on the other hand, has now made it a rule never to drive to her presentations and workshops because she finds driving a stressful and unreliable method of transport. She has made her life even easier by asking for transport to be arranged in advance to take her to and from railway stations.

When we share these kinds of examples on our workshops we can see people's eyes brighten; they then begin to recount similar encouraging stories. Immediately the tone of the workshop changes. It is more positive because ideas (however simple) have begun to flow and people have become more open to receiving them.

There is a growing body of opinion that the more people you know, the greater the possibility that somebody will be able to provide you with something that will increase your resources easily and without cost. The 'in' jargon for this is called Networking. This is simply a proactive way of extending your range of potentially useful contacts. Make it a rule always to carry your business cards or personal address labels around with you. Of course, the reality is that many of these will never be used, but you may need to capture the eye of only one person to acquire the help or advice you need.

It's worth remembering that not only do you have to extend the numbers of people who know you, but you also have to let them know what you need. One of the ways you can make sure people are more aware of your needs is to jot them down on the back of your business card when you give it away (for example – 'I'm looking for cheap computer deal/an office cleaner/a second-hand bike/a buyer for my company/a marketing manager,' etc.). When the person gets back home and goes to file away (or bin!) your card, at least they will once again be reminded of you and what you need.

It may be not be a fair and efficient way of running societies and organizations, but there is no doubt that we do now live in a 'It's not what you know, but who you know' world! So get networking as widely as you can before your resources are so short that you cannot afford the time or money to do so!

ⒺXERCISE

- Take a look at your diary over the next month and mark with one coloured pen the opportunities you have for networking with people who are already known to you and with whom you think you could develop the relationship further.

- With a different coloured pen, mark the opportunities you have given yourself for meeting new people either at home or at work.

- Make a list of up to six current needs which you could broadcast to the world around you in the hope that someone may heed your 'cry for help'.

I USE MY CREATIVITY TO FIND NEW
RESOURCES.

5

REFRAME

In this chapter we show you how to decrease your demands by changing your perception, through using simple Reframing strategies. You will learn how to develop the habit of questioning the way you are thinking about your resources and demands and ensuring that your thoughts are positive but not unrealistic. In short, you will see the glass as half-full, not half-empty.

By far the most common side-effect on perception of having too much pressure is that it becomes distorted in a negative way. (A very small number of people begin to think much more positively than usual. We will discuss ways in which they can help themselves later in this chapter.)

Perhaps you'll recognize some of these automatic reactions when the going starts to get tough:

I'll never be able to cope.

This is a disaster.

She's hopeless – she'll never learn.

I bet it'll rain tomorrow because it is the first day off I've had for weeks.

'Great – still half to go!'

The train is bound to be late – it always is when I'm in a rush.

Given my luck, they won't have it ready anyway.

What's the point, it's bound to be as bad as before.

Oh, no, not another change – that's the last straw.

You'll probably think this is a terrible idea.

Of course everyone has these kinds of thoughts sometimes, even when things are going well. But when we are under pressure the balance between negative thought and positive thought can very easily lean towards becoming unhealthy. Most psychiatrists maintain that a 2:1 ratio in favour of positive thoughts is the normal balance for a healthy mind. We believe that those of us living in the fast lane need to aim one step higher than this and go for a 3:1 balance most of the time.

How Can Positive Thinking Help Us?

A number of people who attend our courses are sceptical about the power of positive thinking. Perhaps this is because some of

'Oh, no – only half left!'

the 'gurus' of positive thinking have been guilty of proclaiming too much on its behalf. We don't, for example, believe that in order to be successful all you have to do is *think* you will be successful. Nor do we believe that all you have to do to build self-esteem and confidence is to tell yourself that you are wonderful and can do it.

Perhaps understandably, the most sceptical people we train are doctors. And, although most of them do admit that positive thinking can have very beneficial effects on health by bolstering the immune system, like them we are not yet convinced by the research done to date that it can reverse inherently physical illnesses such as cancer or heart degeneration. But there is plenty of evidence from research that positive thinking has other considerable benefits.

A study from the University of Illinois investigated whether altering perception has beneficial effects over a long period. The researchers tried to find out if positive or negative thoughts about previous stressful events alter one's perception of future stressful events. They found that positive thinking increases well-being, but for no more than eight weeks. Negative thinking, on the other hand, was associated with lower well-being; the effects of this lasted for more than eight weeks. The study also found that the most important thoughts the subjects had, either positive or negative, were the thoughts they had about themselves.

In a Danish study of 47 anxious patients suffering from panic disorders, it was found that they exhibited far more negative thinking than a group of 30 control subjects (that is, people not suffering anxiety). Thoughts of an anxious or depressive nature were amazingly well related to the bodily symptoms they were having. A further report from the University Medical Center in New York supported the view that negative thoughts and the associated stress reaction were a major factor in skin disorders. It has also been shown that if people with an anxiety and stress reaction prior to public speaking think positively, their stress levels were reduced when compared with those experiencing negative thoughts in simulated public-speaking experiments.

We hope that you will not allow the limitation of current research into positive thinking to put you off, because we do believe from our own personal and professional experience that it has great powers to reduce pressure. We know of one study which showed that optimists practise positive thinking and pessimists do not. Which would you rather be? (The US Olympic wrestling team, who practise positive thinking techniques, know which they'd rather be – and you wouldn't want to argue with them, would you?!)

So, despite some of its limitations we are confident that positive thinking can help you.

Positive Thinking Gives You More Energy

If you think positively, your whole mood lifts. You can energize your body and mind more easily. You feel physically stronger and can think more quickly and clearly. A study done in New York showed that nurses who practised positive thinking were less likely to suffer from burnout than those who did not.

Positive Thinking Helps You Focus on Opportunities

Our senses are highly selective. There is so much truth in the old saying, 'You see what you want to see and hear what you want to hear.' Our brains are continually trying to organize the data that is being picked up by our senses. One of the ways the brain does this is to search for 'matches'. It will select out the data which fits in with our current dominant feelings and/ or the memories we have already stored.

Positive Thinking Attracts Good Support and More Resources

Whom would you rather work or play with – someone who is often in a bad mood or someone who is cheerful most of the time? Whom would you rather lend a month's salary to – an optimist or a pessimist?

Do we need to say more?!

Perhaps not, but we will!

Here's another interesting piece of research found by Malcolm to help reinforce the case for positive thinking. When 82 women with gynaecological disorders were surveyed in Queensland, Australia, the most commonly described personal coping strategy they were found to use was positive thinking.

Why Do Some People Automatically Think in a Negative Way?

There are many reasons why you may have more of a problem in this area than some other people. Your automatic thought patterns could have been established in childhood, in the same way as many of the other unhelpful habits we have already discussed were. Or it could be that you have been spending an inordinate amount of time among negative people. Alternatively, you could be genetically inclined towards depression. Whatever the cause of your negative-thinking habit, the treatment is the same. If you allow it to take hold, you run the risk of becoming more seriously depressed because the biochemistry of your brain will have become firmly set in 'depressed' mode, and the techniques we are going to introduce will not be enough to shift back into normal functioning. You may then need more radical 'treatment' such as drugs, psychotherapy or even a long break away from pressure.

We will now look at a number of our favourite strategies for reframing negative perceptions. These all involve changing your language from negative to positive, whether you are talking to yourself or to others. Doing this will affect your feelings, your motivation and your ability to act in a more positive way.

Reframing Strategies

Positive Self-talk

On our courses we teach people to use *affirmations* as a way of ensuring that they feed their brains with positive, up-beat messages even when the pressure seems too much to bear.

Affirmations are simple positive statements such as:

I am a positive person.

I enjoy challenges.

I can thrive on change.

We are learning fast.

I am organized.

I take care of myself.

I am calm.

We can overcome this setback.

You can also use affirmations to replace self-put-downs as soon as you hear yourself using them, or whenever anyone else tries to put you down. You can say them in your head or speak them out loud. We have found they are much more effective when spoken out loud, even to yourself. Saying them aloud plus writing them down makes them even more powerful. So Billy Bunter's teachers were right when they gave him lines to write out, saying, 'I must eat less cream buns.'

Self-put-down	Possible Affirmations
'How stupid of me.'	'I am highly competent.' 'I've only made one mistake this month.'
'I'm so untidy.'	'I value tidiness.' 'I care about efficiency.'
'Another of my mad ideas.'	'I am creative.' 'I have the courage to take risks.'

Any kind of positive self-talk is better than the negative variety, but we have found that affirmations can be much more effective if you follow these eight basic rules:

1 Use the **first person** ('I' or 'We') statements whenever you can.
2 Use the **present tense**.
3 **Use statements which are believable**, not 'over-the-top' – for example, 'I am an achiever', *not* 'I can achieve anything'.
4 Choose no more than **three or four** appropriate affirmations to say regularly for a set period of time, such as a month.
5 **Write your affirmations out on a card** (preferably decorated and pleasing to your eye!) and keep them in a handy place, such as in your briefcase or handbag, or put them by your bed or on the back of the bathroom door!
6 **Say them regularly** enough to fix them in the memory bank of your brain, but not so regularly that you bore yourself silly with them!
7 **Ensure that you are physically relaxed** when you are saying them. The more relaxed you are, the more impressionable your subconscious brain tends to be. (That's the principle behind hypnosis.)

8 **Speak them aloud** whenever possible and use a positive, calm, assertive tone of voice.

You may be interested to know that self-affirmation has recently been found to help a group of 34 women with HIV. Self-affirmations and affirmations for life were two techniques, helping them to improve their psychological well-being. Affirmations have also proved useful in grief therapy in terminally ill HIV patients, where affirmations helped give them hope and increased their sense of self-worth.

The 'GEE' Strategy

This is a strategy which Gael devised many years ago and which has proved a very useful tool for checking your thinking pattern. It is in fact a simplified version of the very useful psychotherapeutic technique called cognitive behavioural therapy, in which patients are asked to challenge all of their negative thinking. Cognitive behavioural therapy has been shown to help generalized anxiety, panic disorders, depression, hypochondriacal thoughts and even chronic fatigue syndrome, as well as many other psychological illnesses. From 1977 to the present, many good critical studies have shown it to be effective. Some of these studies have shown cognitive behavioural therapy to be more effective than some antidepressant medication.

Although it is by no means a panacea for all psychological illness, the ability to challenge your own thinking to see whether it is appropriate or not, and making modifications to it, is likely to have useful effects. Although it is hard to say for sure whether it is better than other talking therapies, there is certainly more evidence that it works than there is for other forms of talking treatment. Although we would not want Freud turning over in his grave (or rushing, Oedipal-like, to be cuddled by his mum!), the GEE strategy certainly takes up a lot less time and money than three years of psychoanalysis twice a week!

How to Use the GEE Strategy

When you first notice that you are feeling 'down' or over-using any of these kinds of words (which are absolutes or impose limits) – always/never/forever/no one/everyone/nothing/can't/must/should – stop talking (or thinking!) and simply ask yourself the following questions, to see if you have fallen into one or more of the most common negative-thinking habits.

- Am I **G**eneralizing from one or a few specific experiences?
- Am I **E**xaggerating current problems, potential hazards or difficulties?
- Am I **E**xcluding any positive aspects or potential?

Each of these three negative-thinking habits can have the effect of making you view your resources as more depleted than they actually are. If you find that you are generalizing, exaggerating or excluding, you can then Reframe your language.

Generalizing

'Everyone is so stand-offish now-adays.' (This talk may also lead you to think that support is more diffi-cult to come by than it actually is.)

'I am hopeless at interviews.' (You are setting yourself up to fail, and you are not seeing past mistakes as a learning resource.)

Reframe

'Most people are very willing to be friendly. Jane is an exception.'

'The last two interviews I did were not a great success. But I learned a lot from them so this one could be different.'

Exaggerating

'This new procedure is going to cause havoc – you have to be a genius even to read the instructions!' (You are giving yourself extra pres-sure by making a mountain out of a molehill, and are therefore less likely to view the new procedure as a potential time-saver.)

Reframe

'This new procedure is cer-tainly a challenge – but with a bit of time and concen-tration I am sure I will get the hang of it.'

'My boss always asks me to work late.' (Your exaggeration may lead you to resent a boss who obviously thinks you are competent and will owe you a few favours!)

'My boss has asked me to work late for the third time this week. I will have to ask for a review of my terms.'

Excluding

'This meal is a total disaster.' (You go needlessly hungry or don't enjoy the part of the meal which is OK.)

Reframe

'The meat is over-cooked, but it is still edible and there are plenty of vegetables so we won't starve!'

'Jill's a complete waste of space – you ask her to do something, she says "Yes" but then forgets as soon as she leaves the room.' (You risk losing a willing helper.)

'Jill is very willing to help. I could do something to help her remember better and then she could be very useful.'

Malcolm recently used this strategy to help him reframe his irrational negative thoughts when his son asked him for help with his homework. Malcolm had had a highly pressurized day at work and had driven his mother to the shops on his return. He just didn't feel as though he had an ounce of energy left to give to anyone. So his first reaction was: 'Whenever my son asks me to help him with his homework, I never have enough time. I will not be able to relax at all because all my free time will be used up.'

He then became aware that he was generalizing, because the truth was that the request was just for that day. He also realized that he was exaggerating. The truth was that there would probably be at least five hours still left in his evening after helping his son.

Finally, he reminded himself that he had also excluded the possibility of the feeling of pleasure he might get if his son earned an extra House point for the work, or just snuggled up to him on the sofa and said 'Thanks, Dad.'

Through using the GEE strategy as a reframing tool, Malcolm had been able to look at the extra demand on his time and energy in a different way, and immediately his pressure lifted. He felt more in control of his precious resources.

No More Pre-emptive Mind-reading

When we get into negative mode, we often don't ask for the help we need because we have decided in advance that the other person won't want or be able to help us. We must learn to look out for phrases such as the following, which may indicate that we are engaged in 'pre-emptive mind-reading':

> She always looks busy. I'm sure she'll think she hasn't got time to come.

> He'll probably think it's not his job to give me advice.

> What's the point of asking them? They're too young to take an interest.

If you find yourself doing this, resolve to ask for help in an assertive manner. Give the other person the responsibility of saying 'No.' If you need to be doubly sure that you are not imposing, give them an 'easy get-out' by saying something like:

> If you are too busy, I will understand and try to find someone else to help.

> If you do not think it's a service you can offer, please don't hesitate to say no.

> If you are not interested, I'll try someone else.

And remember, don't be tempted to let your pre-emptive mind-reading and anxiety set you up for potential rejection by saying something like:

> I'm sure you'll be too busy, but I'll ask anyway.

I'm sure you have many more important things on your mind, but could you . . .

I don't think this is something which will interest you, but I thought I'd send it anyway.

Challenge Negative Judgements

Negative thinking often leads us into making sweeping judgements about people. This means we view them as much more demanding (or even potentially helpful) than they actually are.

Negative Judgement	Reframe
'She seems very untrustworthy.'	'What evidence do I have? She has let me down once. I must find out if she has let anyone else down and if this is a regular behaviour.'
'Doctor's receptionists are terrible, aren't they? They think they own the doctor's diary. I doubt very much whether she'll give me an appointment today.'	'She may be understanding if I explain my symptoms and schedule for the week. I could ask her to have a word with the doctor, at the very least.'

Replace Prophesies of Doom with Positive Risk Analysis

Prophesying failure not only makes it more likely – because, as we said earlier, it makes you perceive the threats and not the opportunities – it also loads you down with needless anxiety. A much more encouraging method is to talk about any risks in a positive way.

Doom-laden View	Reframe
'The chances are that this won't work any better than before.'	'There is a 70 per cent chance that this will work better this time, now that we have altered the plan.'

'The council may refuse us planning permission.'

'The council turned down 15 out of 100 applications last year, so we have a good chance of getting the plans approved.'

Replace Worry with a Contingency Plan

Worry is certainly a demand that we can control, although many people think they can't. How often have you heard people say, 'I can't help it, I'm a worrier' or 'I can't stop worrying.' One of the best ways we know of stopping worrying is to convert that energy into some constructive contingency planning.

Worry

'I'm worried that there won't be enough material to complete this.'

Reframe

'If there isn't enough material to complete this, I will I have to buy some more.'

'I am concerned that he may not be up to taking on all that responsibility.'

'I had better monitor his progress carefully and ensure that someone can help him out if it becomes too much for him.'

'The weather was so bad, I spent all last night imagining her plane crashing.'

'I will watch the next weather report, and if the forecast is still bad I will ring the airline and ask if there are any problems with the flights.'

Substitute Experience for Guilt

Another pressure we have control over, but again often think we haven't, is our guilt. This emotion (like all emotions) has a positive function, which most of the time we choose not to see. When we feel guilty, we feel oppressed and powerless. Reframing can help us to use guilt more constructively. We can use it as a motivator to help us learn from our mistakes.

Guilt	Reframe
'I'm late again with the figures. I feel terrible. I don't know what they will think of me.'	'Missing this deadline has certainly taught me something about the way I am managing my time at the moment. I will apologize and let him know that I am using it as a wake-up call.'
'I can't stop blaming myself for losing my temper. I feel so bad – she was only trying to help.'	'I am at fault for losing my temper. I have learned that I need to relax more. Now, instead of wallowing in my guilt, I will find a way of making amends.'

Deflect Criticism with Inner Self-defence

When we are in negative-thinking mode, we have a tendency to absorb criticism even when it is undeserved or 'over-the-top'. Some people go one step further and add to the hurt by giving themselves a hard time as well. The following example illustrates how this can speed up the descent into further negativity.

> Brian arrives at the office in a negative mood. He has had a row with his wife the night before and slept badly. At the project review, he is a bit over-confrontational with a member of the IT department about their general lack of support. His colleague Richard is annoyed.

RICHARD: 'You've done it again. You're always putting your foot in it. Why don't you just shut up and say nothing? You always make things more difficult.'

BRIAN: 'I know I upset him, but I was only trying to help. I thought he ought to know what happened last week. I seem to have a great skill for upsetting people. My wife will tell you! I'd better lay low for a while as far as IT are concerned. I bet they'll be even less co-operative now.'

RICHARD: 'Yes, you keep out of it. In fact, keep away from the office for a while, you'll depress us all in that mood. You are probably scaring the customers away, for that matter. Why don't you take a long break?'

BRIAN: 'Yes, I'm stressed out. I don't know if I can cope much longer. If I quit this job, though, it'll only get worse. There's the mortgage to pay and the kids. But I'll probably get the push anyway – then my wife really would leave.'

When you're on the receiving end of any kind of criticism, try whenever possible to reframe it. You can do this with some internal positive self-talk before responding. If you can't do it at the time, certainly do it soon afterwards. This will help you to respond assertively instead of in a passive or aggressive way. It will also put you in a better frame of mind for following it up with constructive (rather than self-sabotaging) action.

This is the kind of reframing talk which Brian could have given himself after Richard's onslaught:

I did behave in a way which I regret. But thank goodness I can rescue this situation with an apology. It has shown me just how stressed I am, and how disturbed I was about my row with Julie even though I thought I wasn't. I need to sort this out with her tonight, otherwise I will lose everything I value.

I USE POSITIVE LANGUAGE TO SUPPORT
MY OWN SELF-WORTH.

Turn Setbacks into Opportunities

Setbacks are another danger zone for negative thinkers. It is hard for most people to view these as potential opportunities, but especially hard for those of us programmed with automatic negative responses. Both of us have made great progress in this field and now find ourselves automatically reframing. For example, last week Malcolm had an important business meeting which was to have given him the opportunity of a large consultancy contract. When it was cancelled, his first reaction was to be disheartened that this opportunity had gone. But within minutes he was able to feel pleased that his day had become less pressurized. He began to list all the advantages:

Now there'd be time to sit down with his secretary and clear his desk.
There was space in his diary and an opportunity to write a chapter of his new book.
He was now able to leave work early and go and pick up two of his children from school.
He would be able to prepare better for the rescheduled business meeting.

Suddenly, not only had 'the disaster' disappeared, it had became a source of opportunity and real enjoyment.

Similarly, last week Gael was to deliver a lecture with another presenter, but the other presenter cancelled at the last minute. Gael's initial thought was disappointment, but almost immediately she decided to seize this opportunity to try out some new exercises.

I TURN SETBACKS INTO SUCCESSES.

Accept the Pressures You Cannot Change

Although the main purpose of this book is to help you feel more empowered in relation to your pressure, we know that there are many demands on your time, energy and emotions which cannot be changed. Nevertheless, many people waste their own precious resources by talking negatively about these. Once they have started on this track, it rolls along – often supported by other negative thinkers around them. This is how it often goes:

This weather is terrible. Isn't it depressing? Why do the weather forecasts always get it wrong? As if I hadn't got enough problems without getting soaked through every five minutes . . .

They've cancelled the 8.40 train. I'll be late – isn't it awful? The train companies nowadays don't care. You can spend all day standing on a platform and no one seems to notice. They said there's been an incident on the line – but there's always something. I get so furious . . .

They appointed a new director again who is half the age of most of us who work here. It's stupid – why do they do it? It didn't work last time – nobody took her seriously. No doubt they'll . . .

Next time you find yourself having or joining in on one of these conversations, why not instead stop, put your hands together and try our 'affirmation version' of the well-known Serenity Prayer?!

> I ACCEPT THE THINGS I CANNOT CHANGE.
> I HAVE THE COURAGE TO CHANGE THE
> THINGS I CAN CHANGE
> AND I HAVE THE WISDOM TO KNOW
> THE DIFFERENCE.

But seriously, this affirmation, said quietly to yourself, can truly help to reframe your perspective.

❸XERCISE

Think of an occasion when you recently felt over-stretched and started to think negatively.

Write a Script for yourself using positive self-talk, making use of all the appropriate above tips and strategies as a guide.

I AM A POSITIVE THINKER

6

RENEW

Our final **R** sounds, perhaps, the easiest of all. It doesn't require that you learn any new theory or techniques. You simply have to increase your enjoyment of life!

We suggest that during times of increased pressure you need to do more (not fewer!) activities which renew and refresh your:

spirit
motivation
zest for life
sense of fun
creativity
curiosity
thirst for adventure
enjoyment of challenge
interest in human nature
wonder at the universe.

In your experience, is this easy to do when the heat is on?

Of course not. It is perhaps one of the hardest tasks we are giving you! When we are under pressure, renewal activities are likely to be relegated to the bottom of our agendas or completely ignored. First, there never seems to be enough time to do them.

Secondly, we never seem to have the energy they may require to organize them. Thirdly, we may have forgotten how much we once enjoyed them!

What Is a Renewal Activity?

This could be the subject of an encyclopaedia, the possibilities are so endless. But to give you an idea of the kind of activity we have in mind when we talk about renewal, we have listed some examples below. We have included our own favourites, mainly to show how one person's choice can differ from another's – even if they are the best of mates and enjoy working together. Gael cannot imagine ever getting a buzz from Bart Simpson, while Malcolm recoils in horror at the idea of curling up with a Tolstoy novel!

Many of these activities are commonly classed as hobbies, but of course they may not inevitably be so for everyone. They may in fact be 'necessary evils' for some people – either a way of earning a living, saving money or pleasing someone they need to please. But equally they could be 'necessary pleasures'. The fact that an activity is something that you *have* to do, or are paid to do, doesn't and shouldn't prevent it from having renewal power.

Gael's Favourite 'Renewals'

- reading novels
- listening to or watching opera
- going to the theatre
- dancing the Argentine tango
- walking my dog by the river or the sea
- chatting with friends while eating delicious food or drinking a glass of superb Rioja wine
- curling up on the sofa and watching TV or videos with my family
- listening to philosophical debates on the radio
- visiting modern art galleries

- swimming in a warm sea under a brilliant blue sky
- learning about an exciting new idea or technique in my field of work
- having a one-to-one with anyone who stimulates me to develop an idea or think differently

Malcolm's Favourite 'Renewals'

Malcolm defines a renewal activity as any task, event, experience, pleasure or time which enables him to refresh his creative and achieving potential, as well as those which reaffirm his joy of life, sense of pleasure, relaxation or achievement. For him a hard day's work which completes a task which he has found difficult, or one which produces work which leads to receiving some praise from clients, colleagues, friends or family, or sets the foundations of future success or contentment are often better than a three-week holiday or a shopping spree in Milan or Paris. They have to be self-contained events in which far more is achieved than he would have thought realistic in a short period of time. They should not use up a precious resource or be the foundation of future problems. Thus long holidays are not 'renewals' for him, because the work is always there to be done when he gets back, he is away from his support structures and they use up two precious resources: time and money. Nor are expensive shopping trips renewing for him, because there is always the guilt (and the credit card bills!) to come home to.

So, a renewal activity for Malcolm usually involves one of three different end-points: clearing up tasks from the past (so that there is a new playing field on which to develop the present and the future), having an enjoyable time using up a minimal amount of energy, time or resources in the present, or laying the foundations for future success.

Malcolm's 'Clear-up Renewals'

- getting my accounts up to date
- writing an article which is long overdue

- using a guide book to value my collection of books, antiques or collectibles
- writing letters to friends I've not been in touch with for over a year
- re-writing my CV
- writing a letter to my father, who died over 20 years ago

Malcolm's 'Present-tense Renewals'

- collecting and finding anything to do with Mabel Lucy Attwell, *Alice in Wonderland*, Arsenal football club or Bart Simpson
- going to a pop concert or football match by myself
- having a meal with a nice bottle of wine, fresh fish, pasta and salad, by the sea in the open air, in the sunshine with music playing
- reading alternate pages of a book with my 8-year-old daughter
- walking around a car boot sale with my 15-year-old son
- going to alternative comedy clubs with my 17-year-old son
- going out for lunch with my 14-year-old daughter and buying her winter wardrobe
- listening to Mahler's *5th Symphony*, Dire Straits, Ritchie Havens or The Doors
- driving in the country in a convertible (I used to like smoking a cigar as well, but have now given this up)
- sailing in the open sea with just the right amount of wind
- lying by a swimming pool watching my children play in the water
- listening to open-air music at a Kenwood concert with a wonderful picnic

Malcolm's 'Foundation Renewals'

- planning a marketing campaign for a new venture
- sending a questionnaire to old and prospective clients to identify their needs and wants

- preparing and mailing press releases to 1,000 journalists
- joining a new tennis club
- finding a personal trainer
- crossing out one morning per week in the diary to make time for fitness training

Here are yet some more examples of Renewal activities which other people we know use with great success:

sports
crafts
travelling to new places
revisiting old haunts with pleasurable memories
painting
creative writing
acting/producing
singing/playing a musical instrument
going to concerts
composing
charity work
political activity
praying
roller-blading with the children
home improvement
workouts
gardening
cooking
collecting stamps/antiques
new adventures: flying in a helicopter/paragliding
making beer/wine
building boats
renovating cars
housework (seriously, some people love it!)

Why Is Renewal So important?

You probably know the answer to this question already. It should be fairly obvious to anyone who has persisted in reading this book, but if you need a gentle reminder before you feel impelled to give these kinds of activities more priority in your life, here it is!

Engaging in enjoyable activities stimulates the production of endorphins and increases our serotonin levels. As a consequence, when we return to cope with our pressures we are much more likely to find that:

We have renewed energy and are holding less tension in our
    bodies.
We see the positive potential instead of the depressing aspects
    in problems and challenges.
We notice opportunities as well as the dull routines.
We feel more positive towards people, so our relationships
    improve and become more supportive.
We trust people more and are willing to ask them for help or
    delegate tasks to them.
We are more self-nurturing towards ourselves.
We feel less compelled by our bad habits.
We are more open to change.

– In short, we become more *Positive Under Pressure!*

Perhaps you can remember your feelings and experiences after a brilliant holiday or receiving some unexpected good news. Perhaps you can also remember these feelings wearing off all too rapidly, and the disappointment (and cynicism) when the pressure started once again to feel unbearable.

As someone who is now committed to living in the fast lane and staying consistently positive under its demands, you will have to ensure that you are giving yourself a constant and adequate supply of Renewal time. You cannot afford to wait for your annual holiday or even the weekend. You must find a way of programming renewal activities into your life on an everyday basis.

I COMMIT MYSELF TO MORE ENJOYMENT.

❷XERCISE

- Make a list of your own 20 favourite ways of finding renewal.
- Mark those which you have given yourself in the last month.
- With a coloured pen, mark those which you've experienced in the last six months.
- With another colour, mark those which you have not experienced in the last year.
- Add six new renewal activities (however small or big!) that you would like to try during the next year.
- Write down up to 10 renewal activities you will give yourself during the next week (at least one for each day).
- Show this list to a friend or pin it up in a conspicuous place.

I HAVE PLENTY OF TIME TO HAVE FUN.

APPENDICES

YOUR OWN
POSITIVE UNDER
PRESSURE
ACTION PLAN

We hope that you have enjoyed reading this book and have found some new ideas to help you manage your pressure. But we hope that you won't now put it aside and just hope that its 'medicine' will get to work on its own. The truth is that unless you do something more in the immediate future about changing yourself and your life, any learning and motivation will rapidly disappear. The next few weeks are particularly vital. We suggest that, as soon as possible, you should sit down with this book for an hour or two and design a *Positive Under Pressure* programme for yourself. Ideally this would be an action plan for the next six months but, at the very least, you should set yourself some easily achievable goals for the next month. The outline plans on pages 181–184 will make your task easier. (Yet another resource to ease your pressure!)

Finally, we should like to wish you the best of good luck, especially during this crucial next phase of your life. Although we are firmly convinced that each of us is ultimately responsible for our own happiness and peace of mind, we know how randomly and unfairly fate sometimes distributes its cards. We have both felt the sense of hopelessness that often accompanies a setback which is not of our own making, especially when it arrives just when we are making enormous efforts to help ourselves. If this happens, be kind to yourself and make sure that you take extra support from people who truly care about your health and welfare. And of course, remind yourself constantly that pressure and stress do not automatically go hand in hand. You do not need to give up your life in the fast lane if you enjoy its thrills and rewards. You simply have to rebalance your demands or resources and become once again:

Positive Under Pressure!

ENDNOTES

Pressure Leads to Pleasure

Laying the Foundations of Change

Stress-beaters: 'The Six Rs'
RELAX – NOTES

Stress-beaters: 'The Six Rs'
REVIEW – NOTES

Stress-beaters: 'The Six Rs'
REFUSE – NOTES

Stress-beaters: 'The Six Rs'

RESOURCE – NOTES

Stress-beaters: 'The Six Rs'

REFRAME – NOTES

Stress-beaters: 'The Six Rs'
RENEW – NOTES

Outline for My *Positive Under Pressure* Action Plan

My Goals for the Next Six Months

In order to manage my pressure more efficiently and avoid stress, I will make the following changes and give myself the following rewards:

1st Month

Behaviour change:
Lifestyle change:
Reward:

2nd Month

Behaviour change:
Lifestyle change:
Reward:

3rd Month

Behaviour change:
Lifestyle change:
Reward:

4th Month

Behaviour change:
Lifestyle change:
Reward:

5th Month

Behaviour change:
Lifestyle change:

Reward:

6th Month

Behaviour change:
Lifestyle change:
Reward:

Signed:
Witnessed:
Date:

My Positive Under Pressure Programme

Month Commencing:

My Early Warning Signals

Physical:
Emotional:
Behavioural:
(See pages 56–65)

My Top Three Priorities This Month

1
2
3

To Respect These Priorities I Will Refuse to:

1
2
3

And Will Say 'Yes' More Often to:

1

2

3

(See pages 111 and 161)

My Three Affirmations for the Month

1

2

3

(See pages 149–150, or choose any of the highlighted statements in this book – or make up your own!)

To check that I Am Thinking Positively, I will:

(See pages 149–160)

Relaxation Techniques I Will Use This Month

Hourly physical 'quick fix':

Daily deep relaxation:

Mind relaxation:

(See pages 71–92)

My Renewal Activities

1

2

3

(See pages 161–167)

To Review My Progress This Month, I will:

(See pages 93–110)

Signed:

Witnessed:

Date:

FURTHER READING

Tony Buzan, *Make the Most of Your Mind* (Pan, 1988)
Richard Carlson, *Don't Sweat the Small Stuff at Work* (Hodder and Stoughton, 1998)
Patricia Carrington, *The Book of Meditation* (Element, 1997)
John Gray, *How to Get What You Want – And Want What You Have* (Vermillion, 1999)
Carla Hannaford, *Smart Moves* (Great Ocean, 1995)
Tim Hindle, *Reducing Stress* (Dorling Kindersley, 1998)
Robert Holden, *Stress Busters* (Thorsons, 1992)
Bradford Keeney, *The Energy Break* (New Leaf, 1997)
Gael Lindenfield, *Assert Yourself* (Thorsons, 1996)
—, *Confident Children* (Thorsons, 1999)
—, *Emotional Confidence* (Thorsons, 1997)
—, *Managing Anger* (Thorsons, 1996)
—, *The Positive Woman* (Thorsons, 1996)
—, *Self-esteem* (Thorsons, 2000)
—, *Self-Motivation* (Thorsons, 2000)
—, *Success from Setbacks* (Thorsons, 1999)
—, *Super Confidence* (Thorsons, 2000)
James E. Loehr, *Stress for Success* (Random House, 1997)
Raj Persaud, *Staying Sane* (Metro, 1997)

Paul Wilson, *Instant Calm* (Penguin, 1995)

Freda Rose Woolsgrove, *Scentsations* (Pathways Publishing, 1998)

If you would like more information on *Positive Under Pressure* seminars and workshops please contact Gael on:

gael.lindenfield@btinternet.com

INDEX